LOG CABIN

LIBRARY

NEW STORIES OF STARTLING ADVENTURE BY THE BEST AUTHORS

Entered According to Act of Congress, in the Year 1891, by Street & Smith, in the Office of the Librarian of Congress. Entered as Second-class Matter at the New York, N. Y., Post Office, March 21, 1889. Issued Weekly. Subscription Price, $5.00 Per Year. September 24, 1891.

No. 132. STREET & SMITH, Publishers. NEW YORK. 31 Rose St., N. Y. P.O. Box 2734. 10 Cents.

TEXAS JACK

OR,

THE WHITE KING OF THE PAWNEES.

By NED BUNTLINE.

CHAPTER I.

THE SIGNING OF THE WILL.

In France, near Avignon, where the silvery Durance weds the beautiful Rhone, the waters as clear and cold as the eye of a vestal, can even now be seen a monumental glory of those chivalric days when men lived and died in armor—when their

SHOT AFTER SHOT, SO FAST THAT HIS REVOLVERS STREAMED FIRE; TOLD HOW WELL TEXAS JACK KNEW HIS WORK.

BUCKSKIN and Satin

BUCKSKIN and *Satin*

★

The Life of

TEXAS JACK

(J. B. OMOHUNDRO)

Buckskin clad Scout, Indian
Fighter, Plainsman, Cowboy,
Hunter, Guide and Actor.

and his wife. .

Mlle. Morlacchi

Premiere Danseuse
in Satin Slippers

★

by HERSCHEL C. LOGAN

With a foreword by
PAUL I. WELLMAN

★

Published by

THE STACKPOLE COMPANY
Harrisburg, Pennsylvania

COPYRIGHT, 1954
by Herschel C. Logan

All rights reserved

L. C. Catalog Card No. 54-11498

FIRST EDITION

Printed in the
United States of America
by
THE TELEGRAPH PRESS
Established 1831
Harrisburg, Pennsylvania

Dedication

To my family who by their patience,
understanding and encouragement
have made this work possible.

Foreword

THE tendency, perfectly natural, of writers in the limitless field of the history of the Old West, is to dwell on the most celebrated or spectacular figures almost to the exclusion of perhaps equally important though less flamboyant personalities. Yet it is not in the highest peaks of a land that its full topography is expressed, nor is it in terms of the Wild Bill Hickoks, the Buffalo Bill Codys, or the Kit Carsons that the full story of the West is told.

My old friend, Herschel C. Logan, a discerning student of western history, and an author and artist of note, has therefore made an important contribution in choosing for his book the biography of a young plainsman who is relatively less known than some of the other figures of the era, chiefly because of his own reticence, although he participated in many notable events and his actions were often important and worthy of perpetuation on the record.

J. B. "Texas Jack" Omohundro, Confederate trooper, trail driving cowboy, guide and scout in the country of hostile Indians, writer, at times a stage actor, the hero of dime novels, yet always somewhat of a mystery, is herein, for the first time, brought to the pages of history on his own account. The thanks of students of the story of the Old West are due to the author for this contribution on a bright but relatively little known facet of that brilliant pageant.

. . . Paul I. Wellman

Author's Preface

WHILE engaged upon some research in 1951, preparatory to writing an article on the "Royal Buffalo Hunt" for *The American Rifleman* magazine I chanced, quite by accident, to acquire an interesting revolver. On the left side of the frame is engraved the following: "TEXAS JACK COTTONWOOD SPRING 1872." This would be interesting enough for the average person, but to an arms collector of many years standing, it was a thrilling bit of good fortune in that it offered an ideal incentive to delve back into history.

Upon completion of the article, the question as to the identity of the man whose name appeared on the side of the gun became uppermost in my thoughts. Something about it seemed to intrigue and to lead me on in my quest. The results of that search uncovered what to me is a most absorbing story of not only one but two inherently modest young people who preferred to let others bask in the spotlight of public acclaim—even though their own accomplishments were such as to reserve for them a place among the immortals of the plains and stage.

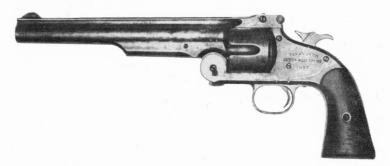

Author's Collection

TEXAS JACK'S OWN GUN
One of Texas Jack's prized possessions was this first model, nickel-plated, Smith & Wesson American revolver of .44 caliber. His name, place and date engraved on the side indicates that it was a presentation piece, given possibly in recognition for services as a scout or guide. The barrel is stamped U. S. and the serial number is 2008.

J. B. "Texas Jack" Omohundro was a true exponent of those plainsmen who contributed so greatly to the conquering of the western wilderness. He left an indelible mark in the annals of the Old West, one which will stand as long as thoughtful people pay homage to those pioneering spirits who helped move the centers of civilization westward.

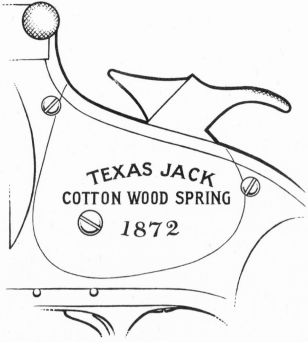

INSCRIPTION ON THE SIDE OF TEXAS JACK'S GUN
This enlarged pen and ink drawing shows, in detail, the engraving which appears on the left side of Texas Jack's revolver.

Mlle. Josephine Morlacchi was born and educated in Europe. From early youth her grace and skill as a dancer had brought her requests to appear before royalty. Being persuaded to come to America in the late sixties it was not long before her quiet and charming personality thoroughly captivated theatre-goers of this country. How our buckskin clad hero of the plains fell in love with, and married, this demure lass clothed in satin and accustomed to the culture and refinement of the old world is but one of the interesting stories brought to light in this research.

It is my feeling that there are still many comparatively unknown characters, such as Texas Jack, whose struggles and triumphs during the frontier days should be recounted again and again. Woven through their lives and deeds are those sterling qualities: honesty, loyalty, vision and self-reliance, which have formed a background for greatness down through the ages. We need ever to be reminded of these attributes in the present onward march of our nation. As long as they are found in our sons and daughters, the spirit of the Old West will live on and on.

The preparation of this biography of J. B. "Texas Jack" Omohundro has been an intensely fascinating experience. The long months of laboriously digging out obscure facts about the young scout, plainsman and actor provided a delightful sojourn into the realm of the historical Old West—a subject which, by the way, has at various times during the past several years afforded me the greatest of enjoyment.

And right here I should like to pause and express my fullest and sincere gratitude to my wife, Susie T. Logan, for her kindly counsel, her patience in interpreting, typing and retyping my pencil scribblings, and for her sympathetic forbearance in permitting me to indulge in the fascinating hobby of Antique Arms and Western Americana—the culmination of which has been this life story of Texas Jack.

It has been my desire to adhere strictly to facts, unembellished by florid coloring, in presenting the extraordinary life of this interesting character. Any deviation from this course should be attributed to an overwhelming desire that you too may come to know and appreciate this sincere scout and plainsman as I have during this intimate study of his colorful life.

Herschel C. Logan

Salina, Kansas

Contents

TECHNICAL GUN BOOKS BY THE AUTHOR:

Hand Cannon to Automatic
   . . . a pictorial parade of hand arms

Cartridges
   . . . a digest of small arms ammunition

1

INTRODUCTORY

Buckskin and Satin

> *How many though, never finish, but mark the trail*
> *with their silent graves, no one can tell. But when*
> *Gabriel toots his horn, the "Chisholm Trail" will swarm*
> *with cowboys. "Howsomever, we'll all be thar," let's*
> *hope, for a happy trip, when we say to this planet,*
> *adios!*
>
> —TEXAS JACK

LITTLE did Texas Jack realize, when he penned the above lines in 1877,[1] that in slightly more than three years he too would be destined to occupy one of the silent graves of which he wrote. Now for the first time the curtain is to be drawn aside, revealing to the world the remarkably colorful life of a modest young plainsman, Indian fighter and showman, and the life of a remarkable woman, his wife, who was the toast of the East.

Among the galaxy of men of the Old West[2] there are to be found those whose star shines with more brilliance than others. The intervening years may tend to obscure, but they can never actually hide their greatness. When inquiring minds go behind the scenes, the saga of their life seems to burst forth with a new luster. So it is with Texas Jack, one

---

[1] *Spirit of the Times*, March 24, 1877.

[2] The following descriptive tribute is taken from a booklet, *"Romance of the Old West"* by the author.

The "Old West" was more than an epoch, more than any one area, it was that indefinable something which made westerners unique in the forging of a great nation.

Born of the frontiers, with the throbbing of Indian Tom-Toms for a lullaby, it grew strong and virile in an atmosphere of choking dust from

of the truly interesting characters in the days of the western frontier.

Seventy and more years have come and gone since this westerner, by adoption, crossed the plains for the last time to that Valhalla of frontiersmen, from whence none ever returns. Here was a man whose companions and friends read like a Who's Who of the Old West—"Buffalo Bill" Cody, "Wild Bill" Hickok, Gen. Geo. A. Custer, Gen. J. J. Reynolds, Gen. Nelson A. Miles, Gen. Geo. Crook, Maj. Gen. Alfred H. Terry, Maj. Frank North, "Capt. Jack" Crawford, "California Joe" Milner, "Doc Carver," "White Beaver," "Colorado Charley," "Arapahoe Joe" and dozens of others.

To many in this modern day and age, so far removed from the grim reality of the frontier, the name Texas Jack may be but a name. Come then as together we roll back the pages of time to those adventurous days of yesteryear. There in contemporary books, magazines, newspapers and notices of the theaters will often be found the mention of his name among other notables of the time and the name of Mlle. Morlacchi. Seldom do people have as much crowded into a life span as did this mild mannered man in his brief thirty-three years of life and his charming wife who did not attain the age of two score years.

*   *   *

It was but a year or so after the War between the States that a young man, recently from Virginia, but then living in

---

oxen drawn wagon trains. Into its sinews were fused the sweat and grime, the blood and tears of generations of hardy men and women. Breathed into its very soul ·was the integrity, thrift and industry of the ages.

Nurtured by flickering candle light in sod houses and log cabins, tanned by summer sun and hardened by the raw cold north wind of winter, it met force with force, with no quarter asked. Justice was swift and terrible, often accompanied by the aroma of smoking six-guns. Yet no mother with her first born could be more tender when the occasion demanded, for beneath a rough exterior there was a heart of gold, attuned to a divine creator.

Tempered in the cauldron of hardships, Indian raids, grasshopper plagues, prairie fires, drought and warfare, it became a challenge to those who produce music, literature and art. Here were born priceless heritages to be handed down from generation to generation. Here was America at its best!

Texas heard of a meat shortage in Tennessee. Employed as he was on a cattle ranch, he conceived a daring scheme, one which, if successful, would help to alleviate the shortage of meat, and, at the same time place a few well earned-dollars in his pockets.

Employing several cowboys and helpers, he started northeastward with a large herd of cattle. The long trek of several hundred miles held no fear for him, for he was thoroughly accustomed to the hard rigors of outdoor life.

Little is known of the trip itself. From meager accounts, however, it seems that some of the men met death and many head of cattle were either killed or stolen by marauding bands of Indians and wild animals.

The Dr. G. L. Howe Collection
TEXAS JACK
(John B. Omohundro)
From a stereoscopic photograph made in 1873 by the celebrated Gurney of New York. It is considered the finest portrait ever made of the youthful scout.

Weeks later the inhabitants of a small town in Tennessee were thrown into an ecstasy of excitement when word came that a herd of cattle was being driven that way. Here was meat on the hoof! Their appreciation was expressed by a rousing welcome to the drivers. When officials of the city asked who was in charge of the cattle, they were doubtless nonplused to see a pleasant young man approaching.

"Where y' from?" asked one.

"From Texas, sir," came the reply.

"What's the name?" called out another.

"Jack, sir," was the only answer.

"Texas Jack, eh?" came a rejoinder from one of the crowd, only to be caught up by loud cheers from the townspeople, "Hurrah for Texas Jack!"

Thus does a newspaper account,[3] at the time of his death, record how J. B. Omohundro, the youthful scout then recently from the command of General J. E. B. Stuart, came by the nickname of "TEXAS JACK"—a name that was to follow this intrepid plainsman the rest of his life.

Nicknames in those days were the order of the day rather than the exception. It was nothing unusual to pin an extra appendage on to a man's name to set him apart from the crowd. Sometimes it had to do with the state from which he came, again it may have referred to his prowess in a certain field, or perhaps it was from some unusual physical peculiarity. Whichever the case, if it struck the fancy of the gang at that particular time, it was usually permanent.

Maj. John M. Burke, who had several years of close association with Texas Jack, later wrote[4] that the nickname was given to him, "after service as a ranger in the Lone Star State," at the time he first met William F. "Buffalo Bill" Cody in western Nebraska. Beyond these two versions there is no actual record of how Texas Jack received the name which he was later to make famous throughout the country.

[3] *Leadville Chronicle*, June 28, 1880.
[4] Major John M. Burke in *"Buffalo Bill, from Prairie to Palace."*

2

BOYHOOD IN VIRGINIA

JOHN BURWELL OMOHUNDRO, Jr., for that was Texas Jack's real name, was the fourth child of J. B. and Catherine Baker Omohundro of Fluvanna County, Virginia. He had four sisters and eight brothers, the youngest of whom is still living. He is Malvern H., of Goochland, Virginia, a half brother. Even though but a small lad at the time, he recalls quite well when his famous brother was the main topic of conversation in the family circle and among friends. The father, "Roaring Screamer," had been engaged in a successful mercantile business at Wilmington for a number of years previous to his purchase of a large plantation near Palmyra, Virginia, just before the birth of the son who was to bring notoriety and distinction to the Omohundro name.

John, or Jack by which name he was best known, was born at "Pleasure Hill" a short distance west of Palmyra, Virginia.[1] In the old family bible is recorded the date of his birth, July 26, 1846.[2] Of his early life, only the most fragmentary accounts are available. From these and from the writings of those with whom he was associated later in life, it is possible to get a sketchy portrayal of his childhood.

His boyhood followed the usual pattern for the youth of that time, with but one notable exception, his love for the great out-of-doors. This was the one dominant trait. Schools, and he was educated in the public schools of Fluvanna and under a private tutor at home, were something to be tolerated only when he found it impossible to go hunting, fishing or horseback riding. While still a lad, Jack became known

---

[1] *The Omohundro Genealogical Record* by Malvern H. Omohundro, Staunton, Va., McClure Printing Company, 1950-51, pp. 512.

[2] Correspondence with Malvern H. Omohundro, Goochland, Va.

around the countryside as a skilled horseman and fearless rider. It was said of him that he was one of the finest shots with either rifle or revolver in the county and that he would bring in game when others would return empty handed. Even as a youth, the spirit of adventure was in his blood, and the possibility of danger seemed never to enter his thinking. It is understandable then that on occasion the call of the outdoor life would cause the boy Jack to play "hookey" from the classroom and to turn to the rivers, the woods and the hills from which he learned so much. It was his contact with nature in those early years that gave to him a natural self-reliance, a characteristic which was to stand him in good stead in later years as a scout for the Confederacy and as an Indian fighter on the Plains.

In ancestry Jack was a direct descendant of Richard Omohundro who settled in Westmoreland County, Virginia, some time prior to 1670. Since he settled among those of English extraction and married an English lassie by the name of Ann Moxley, it has been generally thought that the Omohundro family was of English origin. However, there are some who feel that, because of the "dro" ending of the name, there must have been a bit of Spanish influence somewhere along the line. One thing does seem certain, they were of a noble blood, even perhaps from royal lineage.

In speaking of Texas Jack's ancestry, Major Burke said that Jack was a direct descendant of the Powhatan Indians. It will be recalled that this was the tribe of Pocahontas of Colonial fame. Buffalo Bill, in a tribute to Jack, also referred to his proud and noble birth and of the Indian blood in his veins.

A personal interview with Jack has only recently come to light which verifies the statements of his two friends, Cody and Burke. While in New York in 1877, he was interviewed by a writer of *Spirit of the Times*.[3] His mother, Jack said, was a French lady and a most beautiful one at that. His father, he insisted, was of a grand tribe, the Powhatan, though

---

[3] *Spirit of the Times*, April 14, 1877.

TEXAS JACK AND HIS BROTHER

Earliest known photograph of Texas Jack is this one taken in the early sixties with his brother, O. C. Omohundro, an officer in the Confederate Army. Shortly after this Jack himself enlisted in the service.

just how much Indian blood came from this side of the family he failed to state. Suffice to say that Jack was extremely proud of the Indian blood, however small the amount, which coursed through his veins. To his Indian background he gave much of the credit for his success as a scout and guide.

A few accounts mention his leaving home while but a mere child, only to be brought back by his father. One writer even had him leaving on a sailing vessel at seven years of age. A most diligent search has brought forth no verification of such boyish escapades. It is believed that they were only a filament of some early writer's imagination and were in turn copied by other authors.

Jack was quite young, however, when he decided to make his own way in the world. He had heard of the growing cattle business in the vast Southwest and it was thither that he directed his way. In this day of modern transportation facilities, it is somewhat difficult to imagine the youthful adventurer setting out alone on the long trek from Virginia to Texas. Equipped with a few utensils for camping, a meager supply of clothing and armed only with a rifle, revolver and knife, his sole companion on the long trip was his favorite pony. His simple meals were cooked over hastily built camp-fires; his bed was but a pallet spread under a canopy of stars.

In none of his writings does Jack enlarge upon his experiences during the journey. All that is mentioned is the bare fact that he was in Texas before the war. This would indicate that he was but a youth in his middle teens when he first visited the Lone Star State.

Such is a brief panorama of the ancestry and early life of the youthful Virginian. While it is sketchy in detail, due to lack of sufficient authoritative data, it does form an admirable background against which many of his later activities are brought into prominent relief. The first of these to appear is his role as a soldier.

3

A SCOUT OF THE CONFEDERACY

WHEN the war clouds lowered in 1861
Jack was working on a cattle ranch in Texas.
It was here that he became proficient as a cowboy, develop-
ing an uncanny dexterity with a lasso, as well as adding more
skill to his horsemanship.

A Virginian by birth, and living in Texas by choice, it
was but natural that his sympathies would be on the side of
the South. His age, however, prevented his enlisting for the
first years of the war. His eagerness to join the Army was
heightened by word from home that his older brother had
enlisted[1] and was even then in the field. No longer could he
restrain himself; he must return to his native state to offer his
services in whatever capacity they might be needed.

It must have been a bitter blow to this adventuresome
youth to be turned down on account of his age, but this
seems to have been the case. Accepting it philosophically, he
sought out Maj. Gen. John Buchanan Floyd, who had been
but recently placed in charge of the militia of Virginia after
having been relieved of his command in the Confederate
Army because of his action in leaving Fort Donelson.

Serving as a "headquarter courier" under General Floyd,[2]
he soon brought attention to himself by his outstanding
ability as a horseman and the aptitude he showed as a scout.
In spite of his success he had an intense longing to be with
Orville, his older brother, who was a 2nd Lieutenant of Co.
G., 5th Virginia Cavalry. Some time after the death of
General Floyd in August of 1863 and with his eighteenth

[1] According to his own account in *The Omohundro Genealogical
Record*, O. C. Omohundro enlisted in 1863.

[2] *Richmond Enquirer*, May 9, 1873.

birthday less than a year away, he again sought out the recruiting officers.

That he was finally successful in his desire to "join up" is borne out by the records in the files of the Adjutant General.[3] The Confederate documents, while most incomplete, do show that Jack enlisted as a private in Co. G., 5th Regiment Virginia Cavalry, Confederate States Army, from his home county of Fluvanna on February 15, 1864. His age at that time was some five months short of eighteen. Jack was happy; at last he was serving not only in the command of the noted General J. E. B. Stuart,[4] but what was of more importance to him, he was in the company of which his elder brother was an officer.

The 5th Virginia Cavalry was part of Gen. Lunsford L. Lomax's Brigade in Gen. Fitzhugh Lee's Division, one of the two divisions under Gen. Stuart's command. Since upon the shoulders of the Cavalry Corps fell much of the heavy fighting in the ensuing months, a word concerning the distinguished generals is in order.

General J. E. B. Stuart, nicknamed "Jeb" by his troopers, was but 32 years of age at the time. He was of massive build and endowed with great physical strength and immense endurance. With a boyish weakness for spectacular uniforms and theatrical appearance, he had somewhat of an ostentatious manner. By training and preference a cavalryman, he proved himself a great cavalry leader. His exploits in the field won for him the plaudits even of his enemies. It was in the early summer of 1863 that Gen. R. E. Lee selected him to head the Cavalry Corps, Army of Northern Virginia, a position he held until his untimely death.

"Jeb" Stuart was intensely loyal to the cause for which he was fighting and to the men of his command. He was an officer who never said, "Go," but rather one who said with confidence, "Come on boys, we're going." He was a deeply

---

[3] Correspondence with the Adjutant General, Washington, D. C.
[4] Gen. D. H. Maury in *"Recollection of a Virginian,"* New York, Charles Scribner's Sons, 1894, pp. 113-114.

MAJ. GEN. J. E. B STUART, C.S.A.

Texas Jack, as a scout, is reported to have delivered a dispatch to Gen. Stuart only minutes before a bullet ended the life of this noted officer of the Confederacy.

religious man, a trait at once evident in the study of his correspondence. He was a stern disciplinarian who expected and received the utmost from his men.

General Fitzhugh Lee, called "Fitz", was in command of a division throughout all the latter campaigns of the war, including that of Gen. Early in the Shenandoah in 1864 where he was wounded at Opequon. From March 1865 until the surrender, Lee succeeded Stuart in command of the Cavalry Corps, Army of Northern Virginia. Perhaps his most important, surely his most noted service, was during the campaigns of 1864. He was wounded at the third battle of Winchester in the early fall.

General Lunsford L. Lomax, like Gen. Stuart, was a graduate of West Point (Class of 1856). From 1863 to 1865 he held a cavalry command in the Army of Northern Virginia. His brigade took part in nearly all of the great battles the last year and a half of the war. At the age of 29 in 1864, he had attained the rank of Maj. General.

There seems to be little available material on the brigade's activities the first two or three months of Jack's enlistment, but with the coming of spring there was to be action aplenty. And, from the South's standpoint the increased tempo did not look too promising. Rations were in short supply and men and horses were showing the effects of the long winter just passed. The war was becoming a serious business.

It is regrettable that no official reports of the Confederate Cavalry for the first part of May are in existence. Actual details of many of the battles during this time are fragmentary.

Grant's new Cavalry Commander, Gen. Phil Sheridan, opened the summer campaign on May 4th in what is known as the Wilderness Campaign. For several days the fighting was intense, much of it being on foot. Todd's Tavern and Mitchell's Shop were important engagements as the intensity of the fighting moved the opposing mounted forces southward towards Spotsylvania Court House.

It was during this period of action that Gen. Stuart seemed to lean heavily upon the younger and fresher men such as

Jack. Contact had to be maintained, messages had to go through, all of which required skill and stamina and a thorough knowledge of the countryside. With these qualities the young scout was admirably equipped. This was his home territory and he knew the country like a book. Throughout the course of the campaigns, Jack rendered invaluable service. Due to his youthful appearance, he was often dubbed "boy scout" by many of the older men in the command. The title, however, was not given in a spirit of jest, because they had learned that no task was too hard or no assignment too difficult for the young Virginian.

It appeared to Stuart that Sheridan might be attempting a circuitous route by way of Beaver Dam Station to Richmond. This was serious, for Gen. Robert E. Lee had an advance base there and not too many troops to defend it. Stuart and his force struck out at once toward the main highway (Telegraph Road). At Mitchell's Shop he and Fitz Lee with Lomax's and Gordon's Brigades joined Wickham. Gen. Stuart's worst fears were realized upon approaching the station when he saw the skies reflecting the flames of burning buildings. Hundreds of thousands of rations of meat and bread went up in the fires, set by panicky guards while Confederate soldiers lay hungry around Spotsylvania.

After destroying a quantity of medical supplies, 100 railway cars and two locomotives, Sheridan pressed on toward Richmond.

Jack and other scouts were sent out to reconnoiter and from them Stuart learned that Sheridan's Cavalry was moving toward Negro's Foot. Immediately Stuart started in pursuit hoping to bypass the Federal Cavalry and place his men between Sheridan and Richmond. Movement was slow; men were tired and exhausted from lack of sleep, and animals were weak from want of sufficient food.

Fitz Lee and Lomax were given orders to move by way of Hanover Junction to intercept Sheridan's path. Weary riders and horses arrived there at 9 p.m. on the night of May 10th. Stuart would have pressed on, but Fitz Lee requested

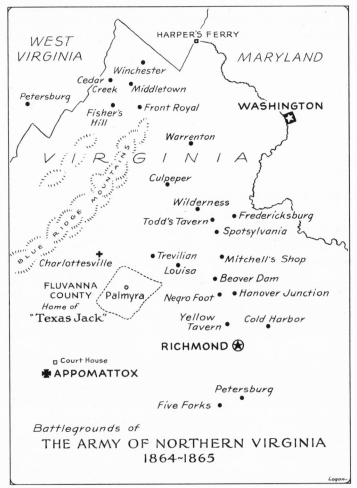

WEST VIRGINIA

MARYLAND

HARPER'S FERRY

Winchester

Cedar Creek

Middletown

Petersburg

Fisher's Hill

Front Royal

WASHINGTON

Warrenton

V I R G I N I A

BLUE RIDGE MOUNTAINS

Culpeper

Wilderness

Todd's Tavern •

• Fredericksburg

• Spotsylvania

• Trevilian

Charlottesville

Louisa

• Mitchell's Shop

FLUVANNA COUNTY

Palmyra

• Beaver Dam

Negro Foot •

• Hanover Junction

Home of "Texas Jack"

Yellow Tavern •

Cold Harbor •

RICHMOND ✪

□ Court House

✹ APPOMATTOX

Petersburg •

Five Forks •

Battlegrounds of

THE ARMY OF NORTHERN VIRGINIA
1864~1865

Logan—

Map showing close proximity of Texas Jack's home to the battle grounds of Northern Virginia.

that the men be given a few hours sleep. Stuart consented with the stipulation that they be ready to march again by one o'clock in the morning.

Eight o'clock the morning of the 11th found Stuart's forces at Yellow Tavern ahead of Sheridan's columns. Wickham was placed on the right with most of the brigade facing the highway. Lomax was on the left with his flank west of and almost at right angles to the road.

In a fierce hand to hand fight Jack's Fifth Virginia beat off the first Federal attack. Being in a vulnerable position Lomax's men were particularly alert during a lull in the fighting. Around four o'clock in the afternoon, fighting broke out again. Taking some of his staff with him, "Jeb" rode to the top of a nearby hill to better view the situation. Heavy artillery fire was demoralizing the gunners there by inflicting heavy losses. Riding among them he tried in his cheerful, confident manner to encourage the exhausted men.

Riding on toward the left with Maj. Venable, he was hailed by a hard-riding young horseman. Lomax had sent Jack with an urgent dispatch for his superior. His men were near the limit of organized resistance and he needed assistance. Though Jack did not realize it at the time, he was handing his beloved commander the last dispatch he would ever receive.[5] Leaving Maj. Venable to assist Lomax, "Jeb" rode on alone for a short distance. A fierce attack sent the Confederates reeling back past the spot where Stuart had stopped by a rail fence. Regrouping, the Southerners roared back in a counter charge. As they did, an unmounted Union soldier by the name of Private John A. Huff (Company E, 5th Michigan Cavalry) took one last shot at the gray-clad figure on horse back. The bullet found its mark and General Stuart slumped in his saddle—mortally wounded.

On June 8th Gen. Wade Hampton received orders to prepare rations for three days and with his own and Fitz Lee's Division to proceed after the enemy. Such preparation involved very little time. The men were given a pound and a half of hardtack and a half pound of bacon; the horses were to have only what corn could be attached to the saddle in a bag.

The night of June 10th found Fitz Lee and his cavalry bivouacked near the Court House in Louisa. Early in the morning Jack was sent by Lee to Hampton to inform him that he was moving out to attack. The battle which ensued was one of those bewildering fights where the attackers sud-

[5] *Richmond Enquirer*, May 9, 1873.

denly discover that the opposition is in the rear. Wade
Hampton discovered this to his dismay. While engaging the
left end of Fitz Lee's line, Gen. George A. Custer's Brigade
broke around Wickham's men. Custer was having a field day
when he found himself amidst Hampton's supply wagons.
However, his joy was short lived. The quick regrouping of
the Confederates all but hemmed in Custer. All supplies were
saved and some Federal supplies captured in the ensuing
engagement.

It is of interest to pause here and to note an important
point which will appear later in the book. Jack, as a young
scout in the Confederacy, was doing his part to oppose the
advance of two Union Generals, Sheridan and Custer—two
men with whom he was to have much contact a few years
later on the great plains of the Middle-west.

In the course of the next few days was waged the battle
of Trevilian Station, which although it resulted in heavy
losses for the Confederates, has, by some authorities, been
regarded as a Southern victory. It was one of the highlights
of the 1864 campaign, along with Stuart's final battle.

It was during this battle that Jack himself received a minor
wound. The records of the Confederate States General Hospital at Charlottesville show that J. B. Omohundro was admitted on June 20, 1864 and then returned to duty.[6]

An interesting story is told of Jack's visit home while in
the Confederate Army, possibly following his medical treatment. It is quoted here the way it appeared in the newspaper
at the time of his death.[7]

. . . in the course of time (he) reached a portion of the country
near his old home, and obtained leave of absence to visit them.
From a stripling boy he had developed into a powerful man,
and his adventures in reaching his home were romantic in the ex-
treme, could space be allowed for detail; in fact his whole life
has been replete with such incidents as dime novel writers love
to elaborate and dish up in sensational form. His family, who
had not heard from him since he left home, were engaged in
festivities in the old homestead, and the darkies were flitting about

[6] Correspondence—The Adjutant General.
[7] *Leadville Chronicle*, June 28, 1880.

in their gayest attire when a man wearing the much dreaded gray uniform appeared coming up the avenue, causing much consternation among the colored folks, who supposed him the advance guard of some awful visitation. But he was recognized by the old family nurse and fear changed to noisy welcome. Every endeavor was made to dissuade him from entering the house, for fear his too sudden appearance would cause the death of the mother who had so bitterly mourned her absent boy. But enter he did, and the effect of the sudden advent of a Confederate soldier, fully equipped, in a parlor where naught but merrymaking was in progress can be easily imagined. All were speechless at the apparition—and it was only when his voice broke the silence with, "Well, anybody here know me?" that normality was restored, and the festivities gained greater zest from the return of the prodigal son. At the expiration of his leave of absence, he made his way back to the Confederate lines . . .

Fighting, though heavy at times, was sporadic during the next two months. The next engagement in which Jack seems to have taken part occurred on the 19th of September at which time Lomax's Brigade fought unmounted. Called the Third Battle of Winchester, it was here that Jack's older brother, Lt. O. C. Omohundro, received his third wound of the war. A bullet in his right ankle incapacitated him for the remainder of the war. At the war's end he was recuperating at the home of his parents near Palmyra in Fluvania County whither he had laboriously worked his way after being wounded.[8]

Within a space of two months Jack was to receive a severe blow. Word reached him at the fighting front that his mother, whom he adored, had passed away Nov. 16, 1864 after a lingering illness. History has not preserved any of Jack's letters, but we can imagine the emotions and heartaches of the young scout at this tragedy in his life.

Plans for Christmas 1864 were interrupted when Lomax's Brigade was alerted by a raid on Gordonsville. The attacking Federal force was driven back without great difficulty and the weary defenders returned to their lines.

The spring of 1865 again saw Jack scouting for Lomax's

---

[8] See *The Omohundro Genealogical Record*, pp. 502.

Brigade. From the last of February until the end of March there were a number of Cavalry raids, although their intensity was considerably diminished.

Like a weak and battered prize fighter whose spirit is undaunted but whose body is completely exhausted, the Confederacy held on in the face of overwhelming odds. Hunger, fatigue, desertions, all had taken a terrific toll. The once proud army of the Confederacy was reeling on its feet.

Then followed the engagements leading up to the war's end—Dinwiddie Court House, Five Forks and finally Appomattox. Jack's last scouting for the Confederacy was done around Appomattox where he was attached to Fitz Lee's Division.

The story of Appomattox is too well known to repeat here. On April 9, 1865, Robert E. Lee surrendered to Grant at Appomattox and the great War between the States was over. Thoughts turned to peace-time pursuits as soldiers on both sides laid down their arms. For many it was a period of restlessness, of uncertainty in adjusting themselves to the reconstruction period.

It was a somewhat bewildered and discontented youth who returned to the old home following the war's end. Having become accustomed to a life of intense action, he found little in the old haunts to intrigue him—the old swimming hole, the hillside paths, all seemed to have lost their appeal. No longer did the throwing of a line into the cool stream or the tramp over the rolling hills with gun and dog bring thrills it once did.

What Jack did not realize at the time was the fact that he no longer was a youth. In age, perhaps yes, but in experience he was far from it. The months on the plains of Texas and as a scout in the army had brought him to mature young manhood.

As the spring days lengthened into summer, the thoughts of the young scout turned again to Texas and its vast cattle ranches. Surely he would find something there to interest his restless spirit.

4

TEXAS CATTLE DAYS

JACK started toward the Southwest and the cattle ranges. How he was side-tracked for a time is best told in his own words: [1]

Immediately after the collapse of one of the great parties to what is styled "the late unpleasantness," leaving Old Bob Lee, and Ulysses to arrange matters, I picked myself up, and lit out with all speed back toward the "Lone Star" State. Reaching New Orleans, I got aboard an old smack that intended to cross the Gulf. As I was in good run of the sour end of luck, a violent sou'-wester struck us, after which the old hulk leaked so badly we had to abandon her, and after a day and night's lively tossing on the "briny," we fetched up standing on the sandy coast of West Florida. The sailor boys struck up the coast to Pensacola, and were soon on deck again, back to the Crescent City, but as I had weakened considerably in regard to "a life on the ocean wave," hearing there was good hunting in the country, and as I had never starved at that business, it being just my long suit, I concluded to camp on the Peninsula, and struck up country to the northwest portion. I soon had an outfit—double barreled shot-gun, ammunition, and salt—and started into the "primitive business," that needs neither wealth in lands, nor capital in money.

Hunting did not occupy all of Jack's time while in Florida. It was here that another unusual facet of his extraordinary life came to light, that of school teacher. This will doubtless come as a surprise to those who have thought of him only as a scout, soldier and cattleman.

An amusing incident to his teaching period is related in one of his writings: [2]

Once upon a time, when I was out in the interior of Florida,

---

[1] *Spirit of the Times*, March 3, 1877.
[2] *Spirit of the Times*, April 14, 1877.

circumstances obliged me to seek the position of school teacher. The schoolmarm was about to retire, and I was anxious to take her place. The young idea is taught how to shoot out there promiscuously, and a he is as good as a she in teaching it. The schoolmarm was said to be of great erudition, and pronounced likely to "smash" any man at "larnin'." I addressed her a letter, in consequence, in which I used the biggest words I could think of. I styled her "honored madam," and beat heavy on "construction," "promiscuous," "retard," the "affinities," and all the ten syllables in general. The letter was profoundly respectful. The next day I was mobbed. The schoolmarm could not read my letter. The big words stuck in the throats of her admirers, and it was with difficulty I persuaded them I meant no harm. They apologized, and I was accepted as teacher. The first day I told the little boys and girls the world was round, and the sun stood still to warm it. The children were amazed. In the evening in came the father of a promising young family, the majority of which flourished amongst my pupils. "What do ye mean by tellin' a lot o' darned lies to my youngsters?" says he. "What do you mean?" cried I. "Why, you idiot, don't you be a tellin' of 'em that the sun sticks stock still, and this 'ere earth goes round him. That's a lie, and you know it. Don't I see the sun a-gettin' up every blessed morning in one place, and a-goin' to bed in t'other, and you idiot you, you keep on a tellin' them 'ere youngsters it sits there all day long, contrary to evidence. You go home, young man. You are dangerous, and 'ill be a-tellin' of 'em I ain't their own father next, you will. Go home, young man." With this, the irate *pater familias* bounced out of the room, sweeping his offsprings before him like the ducklings in a whirlwind.

The duration of Jack's sojourn in Florida is a matter of conjecture. It would appear to have been somewhere around a year's time before he again headed for Texas—this time by land.

There is considerable evidence of his cattle days in Texas, but to pin the happenings down in black and white or to find actual records has been an all but an impossible task. Contemporaries of Jack refer to his Texas days, and, as a matter of fact, he himself refers more than once to them.

Jack's good friend, Major Burke, indicated in his writings, as has previously been mentioned, that Jack had at one time been a Texas Ranger. This may have been possible. Certainly he had those qualities found in the Rangers. Walter Prescott Webb in his book, *The Texas Rangers*,[3] quotes Governor Sam Houston's able description of Texas Rangers:

It is evident to my mind that Texas Rangers stand preeminent on the score of economy and usefulness . . . They are excellent horsemen, accustomed to hardships, and the horses of Texas, having been raised on grass, can perform service without requiring grain to subsist them . . . The Texans are acquainted with Indian habits, and also their mode of warfare. They are woodsmen and marksmen. They know how to find the haunts of the savages, and how to trail and make successful pursuit after them.

They, too, have their families, their kindred, and their neighbors to protect. They have the recollections of a thousand outrages committed upon those dear to them by the savage, to impel them onwards; and if, in pursuit of the foe, they get out of rations, they can subsist on game, being dexterous hunters. What are privations, suffering and danger to them, in comparison with the plaudits of their citizens . . . ? They are accustomed to the heat of the prairies, and the severe northers to which we are subject. They need no tents to shelter their hardy frames from the night winds, but are content with the earth for a bed and a blanket for a covering. Such a force as this, continually on the alert, will be a terror to the savage.

Jack's horsemanship and proficiency in the use of firearms were to prove most helpful on the range. In the locality of the ranch upon which he was employed, Indian horse thieves were wont to make periodic raids. Horses raised for riding and herding purposes offered an attractive prize for the marauding Redskins. More than one cowboy had met death in a vain effort to prevent horses and cattle from being stolen.

Jack was aware of the hazardous nature of his job and he was well equipped and prepared for it. It was not a surprise, therefore, when out on the range one day, shortly after his employment as a ranch-hand, to see a large band of Indians sweeping down upon him and his partner with whoops and yells. But the marauders that day were in for a surprise, for

---

[3] Published by Houghton Mifflin Company, Boston. Used by special permission.

J. B. Omohundro

MALVERN H. OMOHUNDRO

Only living brother of Texas Jack. He still cherishes
fond memories of a visit with his noted brother when
The Scouts of the Prairie played in Richmond, Va.

instead of turning and running, Jack covered the rear while
his partner drove the horses toward shelter. More than one
Indian fell from his horse as Jack poured a deadly accurate
fire into the raiders. Before long they gave up the chase as a
bad job and retreated to lick their wounds and to inquire
in amazement among themselves as to the identity of this
new paleface who had dared, singlehanded, to stand against
them and win. From then on the business end of Jack's rifle
was respected by the Redskins.

Tradition has it that Jack had several brushes with the
Indians, cattle thieves and renegades during his cattle days on
the Texas plains. It was while returning one day from another encounter with hostile Indians that he came upon a
pioneer home which had been ransacked and pillaged but a
few hours before. Nearby lay the still bodies of a young man
and woman, slain defending their home. After inspecting the
scene, and as he was about to mount his horse, his sharp ears

Malvern H. Omohundro

TEXAS JACK, JR., Early 1880's
When but a small lad the parents of this young man were killed by
the Indians. He alone was rescued by Texas Jack, who took him to
Fort Worth and saw that he was placed in good hands. As he grew
to manhood . . . his own name unknown . . . he took the name of
his benefactor in appreciation.

66

detected a slight whimpering sound. Investigation disclosed that before the father and mother had sold their lives so dearly they had hid their four or five year old boy in a small hole under the floor with the warning that he was not to make a sound. When his parents failed to appear after the shouting and shooting had ceased, the little fellow, frightened as he was, could contain himself no longer. It was the muffled sobs that Jack had heard.

Years later, in Charlottesville, Virginia, this young lad then grown to manhood told the story to M. H. Omohundro,[4] an only half-brother of Jack's. He told how Jack had rescued him and how he had taken him to Fort Worth on horseback. Here he was placed in good hands and provision made for his care and raising. Not knowing his own parents' name, the boy in appreciation had taken the name of his benefactor. At the time of his visit with Jack's brother he was with a show troupe billed as "Texas Jack."

Twenty years after the death of his idol, the boy Jack had befriended had become a noted showman. He owned his own circus and had performed in many important cities around the world. In 1903 while the show, "Texas Jack's Wild West Show and Circus," was showing in Ladysmith, South Africa, he was approached by an energetic young man who explained that he was looking for a job and would like to go to work for him. He indicated that he, too, could do a few tricks with a lasso. The youth was promptly hired and billed as "The Cherokee Kid"—later to be admired the world over as America's own Will Rogers.

Will wrote home from South Africa that he had heard of this Texas Jack and wanted to meet him for three reasons: [5]

1. To inquire if he was an American.
2. To find out if he was from Texas.
3. To see, if by any chance, he knew any of his friends in Texas.

He found the answers and stayed with the show troupe for

[4] Letters from Malvern H. Omohundro.
[5] Betty Blake Rogers in "Uncle Clem's Boy" in *The Saturday Evening Post* of Oct. 19, 1940.

TEXAS JACK.
A NOTED AMERICAN SCOUT.

" I was raised among the cowboys, my saddle is my home,
An I l'.(always be a cowboy no matter where I roam ;
And like my noble namesake, my help I'll volunteer,
And try to be of service to the Western Pioneer.

I am a roving cowboy, I've worked upon the trail,
I've shot the shaggy buffalo, and heard the coyote wail,
I've slept upon my saddle, and covered with the moon,
And I expect to keep it up until I meet my doom." —*Texas Jack*.

TEXAS JACK —Born in Texas, he imbued at an early age a love for the wild roving life of the cowboy, and before he was out of his teens had become so proficient in the tricks of the trade that his name became a household word amongst American scouts. Jack has given his remarkable exhibition of expert shooting and rough riding in nearly every city of the world, including San Francisco, Honolulu (Sandwich Islands), Auckland (N.Z.), Sydney (Australia), Java, India, Egypt, Paris, London, and New York.

PROMINENT PEOPLE . . . Texas Jack, Jr.
A page from an English publication entitled "Prominent People." Note how he refers to his "noble namesake" in the verse.

many months. His association with Texas Jack was regarded by Will Rogers as one of the most important periods of his life. He thoroughly admired the skill and experience of the showman from Texas, and in turn Texas Jack took a genuine liking to the kid from Oklahoma. He gave him much attention and help in perfecting new tricks and in polishing up the old ones. Judging from Will's letters home, Texas Jack was a man who never drank, smoked or gambled and preferred that his showmen follow his example. Later in life Will Rogers paid this tribute to his employer and tutor:

Texas Jack was one of the smartest showmen I ever met. It was he who gave me an idea for my original stage act with my pony. I learned a lot about the show business from him. He could do a bum act with a rope that an ordinary man couldn't get away with, and make the audience think it was great. So, I used to study him by the hour and from him I learned the great secret of the show business—learned when to get off. It's the fellow that knows when to quit that the audience wants more of.[6]

Thus does history record how the boy Jack Omohundro befriended, later became the noted showman from whom the matchless Will Rogers said he learned so much. He, too, was a young man, around forty, when the grim reaper struck him down in Kroonstadt, South Africa, in 1905.[7] It is one of the ironies of fate that he also lies in a silent grave, far removed from his homeland.

During these months on the Texas range, Jack further developed his skill as a guide and hunter. To these was added still another achievement—that of a cowboy. He became as proficient with a lasso as he was with a six-gun. One of the finest examples of Jack's writing is a description of the life of a cowboy. For many years, all, or portions, of this classic of range lore was used in the programs issued by Buffalo Bill's Wild West Show. It is included here in its entirety— and from its original source: [8]

[6] Donald Day in *The Autobiography of Will Rogers*, published by Houghton Mifflin Company, Boston, 1949. Used by permission.
[7] Correspondence—Will Rogers Memorial, Claremore, Okla.
[8] *Spirit of the Times*, March 24, 1877.

THE COW-BOY

Philadelphia, March 19, 1877

DEAR SPIRIT: The cow-boy! How often spoken of, how falsely imagined, how greatly despised (where not known), how little understood? I've been there considerable. How sneeringly referred to, and how little appreciated, though a title gained only by the possession of many of the noblest qualities that go to form the more admired romantic hero of the poet, novelist, and historian; the plainsman and scout. What a school it has been for the latter? As "tall oaks from little acorns grow," and tragedians from supers come, you know, the cow-boy serves a purpose, and often develops into the more celebrated ranchman, guide, cattle king, Indian fighter, and dashing ranger. How old Sam Houston loved them, how the Mexicans hated them, how Davy Crockett admired them, how the Comanches feared them, and how much the "beef-eaters" of the rest of the country owed to them, is such a large sized conundrum that even Charley Backus and Billy Birch would both have to give it up. Composed of many "to the manner born," but recruited largely from Eastern young men, taught at school to admire the deceased little Georgie in his exploring adventures, and though not equaling him in the "cherry-tree goodness," more disposed to kick against the bull-dozing of teachers, parents, and guardians.

As the rebellious kid of old times filled a handkerchief, (always a handkerchief, I believe), with his all, and followed the trail of his idol Columbus, and became a sailor bold, the more ambitious and adventurous youngster of later days freezes on to a double-barreled pistol, and steers for the bald prairie to seek fortune and experience. If he doesn't get his system full, its only because the young man weakens, takes a back seat, or fails to become a Texas cow-boy. If his Sunday-school ma'am has not impressed him thoroughly with the chapter about our friend Job, he may be astonished, but he'll soon learn the patience of the old hero, and think he pegged out a little too soon to take it all in. As there are generally openings, likely young fellows can enter, and not fail to be put through. If he is a stayer, youth and size will be no disadvantage for his start in, as certain lines of the business are peculiarly adapted to the light young horsemen, and such are highly esteemed when they become thoroughbreds, and fully possessed of "cow sense."

Now, cow sense has a deeper meaning than it seems to have, as in Texas it implies a thorough knowledge of the business and a natural instinct to divine every thought, trick, intention, want, habit, or desire of his drove, under any and all circumstances.

A man might be brought up in the States swinging to a cow's tail, and, taken to Texas, would be as useless as a last year's bird's nest with the bottom punched out. The boys grow old soon, and the old cattle-men seem to grow young; and thus it is that the name is applied to all who follow the trade. However, inside the trade the boys are divided into range-workers and branders, road-drivers and herders, trail-guides and bosses.

As the railroads have now put an end to the old-time trips, I will have to go back to a few years ago, to give a proper estimate of the duties and dangers, delights and joys, trials and troubles, when off the ranche. The ranche itself and the cattle trade in the State still flourish in their old-time glory, but are being slowly encroached upon by the modern improvements that will in course of time wipe out the necessity of his day, the typical subject of my sketch. Before being counted in and fully endorsed, the candidate has to become an expert horseman, and test the many eccentricities of the stubborn mustang; enjoy the beauties, learn to catch, throw, fondle—oh! yes, gently fondle (but not from behind)—and ride the "docile" little Spanish-American plug, an amusing experience in itself, in which you are taught all the mysteries of rear tear, stop and drop, lay and roll, kick and bite, on and off, under and over, heads and tails, handsprings, triple somersaults, stand on your head, diving, flip-flaps getting left, (horse leaves you fifteen miles from camp—Indians in the neighborhood, etc.), and all the funny business included in the familiar term of "bucking"; then learn to handle a rope, catch a calf, stop a crazy cow, throw a beef steer, play with a wild bull, lasso an untamed mustang, and daily endure the dangers of a Spanish matador, and with a little Indian scrape thrown in, and if there is anything left of you they'll christen it a first class cowboy. Now his troubles begin (I have been worn to a frizzled end many a time before I began); but after this he will learn to enjoy them—after they are over.

As the general trade on the range has often been written of, I'll simply refer to a few incidents of a trip over the plains to the cattle markets of the North, through the wild and unsettled portions of the Territories, varying in distance from fifteen hundred to two thousand miles—time, three to six months—extending through the Indian Territory and Kansas, to Nebraska, Colorado, Dakota, Montana, Idaho, Nevada, and sometimes as far as California. Immense herds, as high as thirty thousand or more, are moved by single owners, but are driven in bands of one to three thousand, which, when under way, are designated "herds." Each of these have from ten to fifteen men, with a wagon driver

and cook, and the "king-pin of the outfit," the boss, with a supply
of two or three ponies to a man, an ox team, and blankets, also
jerked beef and corn meal—the staple food; also supplied with
mavericks or "doubtless-owned" yearlings for fresh meat supply.
After getting fully under way, and the cattle broke in, from ten
to fifteen miles a day is the average, and everything is plain sailing, in fair weather. As night comes on, the cattle are rounded
up in a small compass, and held until they lie down, when two
men are left on watch, riding round and round them in opposite
directions, singing or whistling all the time, for two hours, that
being the length of each watch. This singing is absolutely necessary, as it seems to soothe the fears of the cattle, scares away the
wolves, or other varmints that may be prowling around, and pre-
vents them from hearing any other accidental sound, or dreaming
of their old homes, and if stopped would, in all probability, be the
signal for a general stampede. "Music hath charms to soothe the
savage beast," if a cow-boy's compulsory bawling out lines of
his own composition, such as these:

> Lay nicely now cattle, don't heed any rattle,
>> But quitely rest until morn,
> For if you skedaddle, we'll soon give you battle,
>> And head you as sure as you're born.

can be considered such.

>> Some poet may yet make a hit,
>> On the odds and ends of cow-boy's wit.

But on nights when old "Prob," goes on a spree, leaves the
bung out of his water barrel above, prowls around with his
flash box, raising a breeze, whispering in tones of thunder, and
the cow-boy's voice, like the rest of the outfit, is drowned out,
steer clear, and prepare for action. If them quadrupeds don't go
insane, turn tail to the storm, and strike out for civil and religious liberty, then I don't know what strike out means. Ordinarily, so clumsy and stupid looking, a thousand beef steers can
rise like a flock of quail on the roof of an exploding powder mill,
and will scud away like a tumble weed before a high wind,
with a noise like a receding earthquake. Then comes fun and
frolic for the boys!

Talk of "Sheridan's ride, twenty miles away," that was in the
daytime, but this is the cow-boy's ride with Texas five hundred miles away, and them steers steering straight for him; night
time, darker than the word means, hog wallows, prairie dog,
wolf and badger holes, ravines and precipices ahead, and if you
do your duty three thousand stampeding steers behind. If your
horse don't swap ends, and you hang on them till daylight, you

can bless your lucky stars. Many have passed in their checks at this game. The remembrance of the few that were foot loose in the Bowery a few years ago, will give an approximate idea of three thousand raving bovines on the warpath. As they tear through the storm at one flash of lightning, they look all tails, the next flash all horns. If Napoleon had a herd at Sedan, headed in the right direction, he would have driven old Billy across the Rhine.

The next great trouble is crossing streams, which are invariably high in driving season. When cattle strike swimming water they generally try to turn back, which eventuates in their "milling," that is swimming in a circle, which if allowed to continue, would result in the drowning of many. There the daring herder must leave his pony, doff his togs, scramble over their backs and horns to scatter them, and with whoops and yells, splashing, dashing, and didoes in the water, scare them to the opposite bank. This is not always done in a moment, for a steer is no fool of a swimmer; I have seen one hold his own for six hours in the Gulf after having jumped overboard. As some of the streams are very rapid, and a quarter to half a mile wide, considerable drifting is done. Then the naked herder has plenty of amusement in the hot sun, fighting green head flies and mosquitoes, and peeping around for Indians, until the rest of the lay-out is put over—not an easy job. A temporary boat has to be made of the wagon box, by tacking the canvas cover over the bottom, with which the ammunition and grub is ferried across, the running gear and ponies swam over after. Indian fights and horse thief troubles are part of the regular rations. Mixing with other herds and cutting them out, again avoiding too much water at times, and hunting for a drop at others, belongs to the regular routine.

Buffalo chips for wood a great portion of the way (poor substitute in wet weather), and avoiding prairie fires later, varies the monotony. In fact it would fill a book to give a detailed account of a single trip, and it is no wonder that the boys are hilarious when it ends, and, like the old toper, "swear no more for me," only to return and go through the mill again.

How many though never finish, but mark the trail with their silent graves, no one can tell. But when Gabriel toots his horn, the "Chisholm trail" will swarm with cow-boys. "Howsomever we'll all be thar," let's hope, for a happy trip, when we say to this planet, *adios!*

How many cattle drives Jack made to northern states over

the Chisholm Trail [9] during his nearly three years in Texas are not recorded. From his own writing it is logical to assume that he made several trips into Central Kansas when Abilene was the end of the cattle trail—and "king of the cow-towns."

Even the locale of the ranch upon which Jack worked in Texas is unknown. One early-day writer indicated that it was in the Panhandle, not far from the Indian Territory. Jack himself gives no hint as to the part of Texas in which he lived.

As much as he liked Texas it is obvious that he found something in the prairies to the north which appealed to him. Then, too, with the railroads pushing west across Kansas and Nebraska it was possible to see more of the country on his trips to the great plains. In the summer and early fall of 1869 he spent some time in and around Fort Hays, Kansas. It was here that he met "California Joe" Milner, General George A. Custer's chief of Scouts. Custer and his troops had but recently returned from the battle of the Washita. Milner and Forrest in their definitive book, *California Joe*,[10] describe the meeting of the two scouts in this manner:

[9] One of the best descriptions of this historic old trail was written in 1892 by Charles M. Harger of Abilene, Kansas. It is quoted here with his permission, and that of the Kansas State Historical Society.

From two hundred to four hundred yards wide, beaten into the bare earth, it reached over hill and through valley for over six hundred miles, a chocolate band amid the green prairies, uniting the North and South. As the marching hoofs wore it down and the wind blew and the waters washed the earth away, it became lower than the surrounding territory, and was flanked by little banks of sand, drifted there by the wind. Bleaching skulls and skeletons of weary brutes who had perished on the journey gleamed along its borders, and here and there was a low mound showing where some cowboy had literally "died with his boots on." Occasionally a dilapidated wagon frame told of a break down, and spotting the emerald reaches on either side were the barren circle-like "bedding-grounds," each a record that a great herd had there spent a night.

The wealth of an empire passed over the trail, leaving its mark for decades to come. The traveler of today sees the wide trough-like course, with ridges being washed down by the rains, and with fences and farms of the settlers and the more civilized Redmen intercepting its track and forget the wild and arduous life of which it was once the exponent.

[10] Published by The Caxton Printers, Ltd., Caldwell, Idaho, 1935. Used by their permission.

Selina M. Dermody

CALIFORNIA JOE . . . (Moses Emory Milner)
Custer's favorite scout and one of the most picturesque
characters on the plains. He was a "pard" of Texas Jack
until his death at the hands of an unknown assassin in 1876.

After his return to Fort Hays, Joe made the acquaintance of
that famous scout and plainsman, John B. Omohundro, known
over the West as "Texas Jack." He has been dead for nearly
half a century and many other Texas Jacks have come and gone;
but the name of this noted plainsman who was the partner of
Buffalo Bill and Wild Bill, still survives throughout the land. He
is described as a pleasant man who made friends easily, a man
with a smile and a joke for all, but very dangerous when his
anger is aroused. During the days California Joe spent at Fort
Hays he and Texas Jack became warm friends.

Another significant friendship formed by Jack at this time
was with the marshal of Hays, J. B. "Wild Bill" Hickok.
Even though they had fought under different flags in the
late war, they saw in each other qualities which drew them
together and made them friends for life. It must have been
an impressive sight to the townspeople to see the three scouts,
each over six feet in height, sauntering down the streets of
this early frontier town, for they were much together during
those days.

A visit to the vicinity of North Platte, Nebraska, which Jack made about this time was destined to change the course of his life. The events leading up to, and including his most notable year are told in the next epoch of his fascinating career.

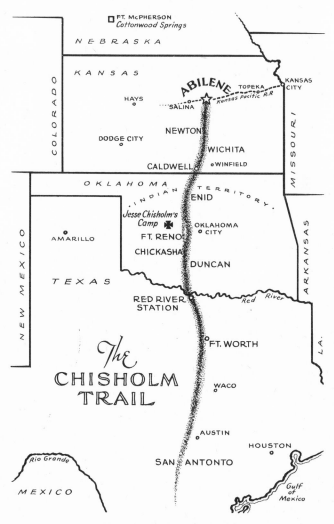

THE CHISHOLM TRAIL

Acclaimed in story and song as the most famous cattle trail of the Old West. It extended from around San Antonio, Texas to Abilene, Kansas, a distance of over six-hundred miles.

"WILD BILL" HICKOK
Numbered among the close friends of Texas Jack was the famous scout and frontier peace officer, James B. Hickok. An assassin's bullet ended his life at Deadwood, S. D. in 1876.

5

COTTONWOOD SPRINGS

ON JANUARY 15, 1860, Charles McDonald settled in a bend of the Platte River some seventeen miles southeast of what is now North Platte, Nebraska. Here he established a ranch and an overland trading post consisting of a store, blacksmith shop, post office and hostelry. A short distance to the northeast of the house, an abundance of clear sparkling water flowed from a spring in the side of a small ravine. Standing like a sentinel by the spring was a lone, giant cottonwood tree. From this combination came the name of this early day trading post—Cottonwood Springs.[1] From the canyon to the south and west

---

[1] Interview with William H. McDonald, North Platte, Nebraska.

COTTONWOOD SPRINGS, 1952

Present-day view of the historic site of Cottonwood Springs. A lone cottonwood tree standing guard over a bubbling spring, which flowed from the bank to the left of the bridge, gave the name Cottonwood Springs to this historic spot.

of the trading post came the red cedar logs for erecting the buildings. From here also came the poles upon which the wires were hung for the first telegraph line stretching out across the prairie in western Nebraska.

Like an oasis in the desert, Cottonwood Springs was a haven for the weary travelers.[2] Here pioneers rested and loaded up with provisions for the long trek westward through Indian infested territory. Scouts and hunters found beneath its shelter a hospitable home base for their operations. Between the post and the spring were to be found the worn trails of the Oregon Trail, the Overland Trail and the Pony Express route. For something like a hundred miles along the Platte River the three trails merged into one. Even today momentos are to be found along the old trails—horseshoes, iron pieces from old wagons, glassware and other items which have survived the years.

Arthur Chapman in his book *The Pony Express*[3] tells of this somewhat unusual happening at Cottonwood Springs:

Some of these places of "rest and refreshments for man and beast" along the way were run legitimately enough; others were refuges for horse thieves and outlaws who prowled along the trail. Occasionally a traveler, who may have foolishly made a display of money, was "done in" and was never heard from again. Complaints about horse stealing were numerous. The fine stock at the Pony Express stations was guarded night and day. Without redoubled precautions under such circumstances, the "Pony" riders would soon have been set afoot.

Horse thieves were shown no mercy. Near the "Pony" station at Cottonwood Springs, the junction of the north and south forks of the Platte, was an enterprising rancher known as "Frenchy," who had his own system of preying on the trail trade. Emigrants who camped at or near "Frenchy's" place would lose valuable horses. "Frenchy" would be all concern on hearing of the loss, but would suggest that perhaps the horses had strayed away. He knew the country well, and for a consideration—no inconsiderable price was named—"Frenchy" would absent himself from his business and try to hunt up the animals. If a deal was made, "Frenchy" would appear with the horses

COTTONWOOD SPRINGS, 1872

Overland and Oregon Trading Post of Charles McDonald at Cottonwood Springs. The post covered an area 75 yards East and West by 100 yards North and South, and was surrounded by an eight foot high red cedar stockade. Texas Jack was often a visitor in this frontier post.

MAP OF FORT McPHERSON
This map shows the location of Cottonwood Springs,
"home" of Texas Jack, in relation to the Fort.

and receive his fee.

Unfortunately for the sauve keeper of the ranch, he worked the same trick twice on the same travelers—once when they were going to the gold fields and again when they were returning. "Frenchy" was found, quite dead, hanging from the upraised pole of one of his own wagons.

In 1863 the War Department, in looking for a site for a military outpost, acted upon the suggestion of Charles McDonald and selected the area of ground upon which Cottonwood Springs was located. On September 18, 1863, Lieutenant George W. Heath of Co. G, 7th Iowa Cavalry, with 20 men arrived at the post. By the 30th of September the entire company, under Captain Elisha Hammer was on the ground. Upon his arrival, Major George M. O'Brien, of the 7th Iowa Cavalry, assumed command and named the camp— Cantonment McKean.

On May 18, 1864, when the camp had begun to take on the looks of an adequate military installation, the name was changed to Fort Cottonwood. Finally, on February 20, 1866, the name was permanently changed to Fort McPherson, in honor of General James B. McPherson, one of General W. T. Sherman's commanders, killed at the battle of Atlanta.

A splendid detailed description of the buildings at this early day frontier fort was given by Assistant Surgeon Charles L. Heizmann, U. S. Army, in circular No. 8 issued by the War Department, May 1, 1875:

The buildings are arranged about a quadrangle 844 by 550 feet. Two sides are formed by five barracks, three log and two frame; one (log, shingle roof) 145 by 27 feet, with wings of 87 by 20 feet; one (frame, shingle roof) (unoccupied and out of repair) 108 by 27 feet, with a wing of 69 by 20 feet; one (log, shingle roof, unoccupied) 114 by 27 feet, with wing 69 by 20 feet; one (frame, shingle roof) 147 by 27 feet, with wing 69 by 20 feet, and another (log, shingle roof) 132 by 30 feet, with no wing. Each building contains eighteen windows, and compartments used as dormitories, orderly-rooms, dining and cooking rooms. The dormitories are ceiled. Average airspace per man in two buildings occupied at present is 698 cubic feet. Single iron beds are used. Ventilation is by window and roof ventilators.

One side is occupied by officers' quarters—frame, lathed and plastered, with shingle roofs—in good repair. Three single buildings, 42 by 20 feet; four double, 54 by 20 feet; one commanding officer's, 65 by 24 feet. Two single buildings, 40 by 20 feet, are on a line with the hospital, in the rear of the main line of officers' quarters. All have kitchens, 24 by 15 feet.

The fourth side is occupied by the adjutant's office, (new), 41 by 30 feet; quartermaster's office, (new), 36 by 30 feet; the commissary storehouse, (new), 96 by 25 feet, with wing 90 by 19 feet.

In the rear of the barracks are the quartermaster's warehouse, (log) 132 by 30 feet; the forage building, (log), 130 by 27 feet; and six laundresses' houses, (five log and one frame), two, 40 by 24 feet; one, 30 by 15 feet; one, 40 by 18 feet, with wing 24 by 15 feet; one, 60 by 18 feet; one, 30 by 15 feet, with wing 12 by 15 feet; also the cavalry stables, log with shingle roofs; four 200 by 30 feet; and one, 235 by 30 feet.

A new guard house was erected in 1874. It is built of logs,

FORT McPHERSON, 1872

A panoramic view of Fort McPherson in 1872 at the time Texas Jack was a familiar figure around this noted military post.

42 by 18 feet, and 9 feet high from floor to ceiling, and contains, besides a guard room, ten single cells, each 6 by 3 feet, and one double cell, 6 by 6 feet. There is no general prison room. Ventilation is sufficient.

The post bakery (log) is 45 by 30 feet, with large oven.

The hospital is a log building, well chinked and plastered, with lathed and plastered ceilings and shingle roof. It consists of a main building 69 by 20 feet, and a wing 56 by 20 feet, forming an "L."

The two ward rooms, respectively 20 by 38 feet and 20 by 20 feet, will accommodate twenty-four patients, giving to each 466 cubic feet air-space. The dispensary is 20 by 12 feet, the steward's room 10 by 20 feet, the dining room and store room are each 20 feet square. The washroom, 8½ by 15 feet, adjoins the larger ward. The steward's quarters have a kitchen 14 by 20 feet, adjoining. The hospital kitchen, 16 by 20 feet, communicates with the dining room in the wing of the building. An addition of a post-mortem room has been made.

The first white child born at Cottonwood Springs was W. H. McDonald, son of Charles and Orra (Henry) McDonald. His birth occurred on June 14, 1861, and at this writing he is the picture of health and is still quite active in the affairs of North Platte. He has been chairman of the

WILLIAM H. McDONALD
Mr. W. H. McDonald of North Platte, Nebraska . . . first white child born at Cottonwood Springs, Nebraska. He recalls quite vividly the days when this pioneer stopping point was "home" to Texas Jack.

board of the McDonald State Bank for many years. His memory of those early days is most remarkable and accurate. It is a never-to-be-forgotten experience to sit down in the living room of his home and to reminisce with him on the frontier days. He is one of the few living men who knew Texas Jack personally, and his memory of the young plainsman is quite vivid. The home of William F. "Buffalo Bill" Cody was but a stone's throw from his birthplace. As a lad, he and Cody's children spent much time together. Later in life he was a friend, confidant and banker for Buffalo Bill during his circus days. His friends have included many of the pioneers who made western history.

Mr. McDonald recalls that it was in 1869 when Jack, in the employ of a Mr. Brown, drove a small herd of Texas longhorns to the vicinity of Cottonwood Springs. Something about the country or the people must have appealed to the young scout from Texas. Perhaps it was the activity in the great mid-West, and there was activity aplenty—Indian raids, buffalo hunts and frontier army life. Here, too, in the center of this sphere of activity were to be found most of the noted men of the Old West, names of prominence even at that time. It is logical that all this offered a special inducement to the young man from the South. From his early life, the love of adventure and the great outdoors had been an integral part of him. To him the great plains beckoned and to them he came.

Nebraska at that time was the scene of much frontier activity. Tracks for the Union Pacific Railroad had, only a few months before, been laid westward across the state. Guides for eastern hunting parties were in demand and Indian depredations were common. It was not always whites against Indians, but many times Indians against Indians. To better understand the Indian situation into which Jack came, a bit of background may be helpful. It will serve to explain some of his later activity.

From available sources it appears that there was considerable friction between the Pawnee Indians and the Sioux and

Cheyennes. For the most part the Pawnees were a permanent tribe, that is, they preferred to build settlements, cultivate the ground, hunt, fish and trap and to generally live at peace with their white brothers, whom they had learned to accept as a necessary evil in the encroachment of their hunting ground. On the other hand, the nomadic Sioux and Cheyennes seemed to take a peculiar delight in warring upon the sedentary Pawnees and early white settlers.

As a protection against the marauding tribes, Major Frank J. North was persuaded to investigate the possibility of enlisting the support of a good number of Pawnee braves into an Indian Battalion. The activities and the success of the celebrated Pawnee Scouts is too well known to be recounted here. Suffice to say that in the years between 1864 and 1877 the Pawnee Scouts wrote an important chapter to the winning of the West.

For some reason the best scouting and work of the Pawnees was done under the discipline of white leadership. Left to themselves, they often became too involved in past customs and personal animosities with other tribes to present a united front against their enemies, the Sioux and Cheyennes.

Most respected by the Indians were those few white scouts whose skill as plainsmen and whose understanding of and sympathy for the Indians set them apart from other pioneers. The life of a scout on the frontier called for the best in a man—ability, skill, resourcefulness in perilous situations and an unwavering courage in the face of constant danger. Such attributes did the Pawnees find in Texas Jack. Here in Nebraska he lived the carefree life of a plainsman, scout and hunter, mingling and trading often with the Pawnee's among whom he made many friends.

His sympathy was with this Indian tribe in its all but lonely fight against its enemies. The handling of the Pawnee problem by the Indian Office officials was but another sordid and disgraceful chapter in the story of the government handling of the American Indians, a chapter which incidentally has continued to this day.

COL. WM. F. CODY
"Buffalo Bill"
Known and beloved the world over as the one and only authentic
"Buffalo Bill" of the Old West.

Jack's companions during those days included Dr. W. F. Carver, later known internationally as the world's greatest rifle shot, Johnny Nelson, (the squaw man), Jim Lauderdale, Monty and Hank Clifford, Arthur Roff and others.[4]

It was at Cottonwood Springs that Jack first met "Buffalo Bill." Being of the same age and with similar likes and dislikes, a close friendship soon developed between the two plainsmen. At the time of their meeting, Cody was already widely known on the frontier. During the building of the Kansas Pacific Railroad through Central Kansas in 1867-68, he had been employed at a salary of $500 per month to supply meat for the construction crews. Affable, genial and withal an expert provider of meat, Cody was a great favorite of the workers. One of them in a moment of jest made up the following jingle:

> Buffalo Bill, Buffalo Bill
> Never misses and never will
> Always aims and shoots to kill
> And the company pays his buffalo bill.

It made an instant hit and from then on for fifty years, the world was to know him more familiarly as "Buffalo Bill." Others have attempted to claim the title of being "the original Buffalo Bill," only to appear in a ridiculous light. The name "Buffalo Bill" did not originate with any of these lesser figures, nor with Cody for that matter. In fact the nickname had been used on the frontier for many years, and, it had even appeared in a national publication as far back as 1846, the year of Cody's birth.[5] The truth is, however, that William F. Cody was the one who, in his own inimitable way, made the name world famous, and today thousands yearly honor him by a visit to his grave—ample proof that he is still beloved as the "one and only Buffalo Bill."

The relationship between Texas Jack and Buffalo Bill was without doubt the underlying reason for the former's decision to bunk down at Cottonwood Springs. Their comradeship

---

[4] Charles R. Nordin in the *Nebraska History Magazine*, Oct.-Dec., 1927.
[5] *National Police Gazette*, Vol. 1, No. 32, April 18, 1846.

was not unlike that of brothers; Texas Jack was like one of the family in the Cody household. Each saw in the other fine qualities to be admired. Much of their time during the next few years was spent together. Truly they were—as Buffalo Bill later said—"pards" of the plains for life, even though the late war had seen them serving under opposite flags.

Two years later, 1871, Jack was to be found acting as a guide, hunter and scout out of Cottonwood Springs. In fact his name and ability seem to have been well established on the plains and among the noted characters of the West. No longer was it John B. or Jack Omohundro, but henceforth America was to know him as "TEXAS JACK."

One interesting incident in which the young plainsman played an important part will bear recounting here. It will serve to illustrate the bravery and fearlessness of Texas Jack at the time he was living at or near Fort McPherson.

It seems that supply wagons bound for the fort were being held up by a band of robbers. After a lightning attack on the supply train, they would vanish into the hills and successfully elude any parties sent out after them.

Something in the nature of their disappearance must have intrigued Jack, because he took it upon himself to see what could be done to put a stop to such depredations. It was not long until close observation directed his suspicions to a locality not too far from the fort. Here he noted some strangers, loafers and gamblers who did not appear to fit into the pattern of life around those parts.

Changing his name to Dave Hunter and adopting a different manner of dress, Jack began to frequent the gambling houses where the strangers loitered. One method in those days to strike up a conversation quickly was to step up to the bar and call for drinks for the crowd. Following this custom now and then for a few days, he had little difficulty in engaging his suspects in friendly talk. Before long they invited him to sit in on a game of cards "to take a hand for luck" so they said. Even though he was no novice at cards, he figured it the best part of strategy to play it dumb—and lose—which is what he did.

Even though one of the strangers was attired much differently, Jack soon recognized him as the one whom he had seen loitering around a certain bluff in close proximity to the wagon trail leading to the fort. Indeed he was the lookout for the band of robbers. So well had Jack altered his own appearance that it never dawned upon the stranger that the man sitting across the table from him was the noted Texas Jack who had surprised him a few days previously on the road near the bluff.

Before many days had passed the small group of gamblers invited Jack to their home some little distance away. Here they were joined by others until there was a considerable gang of ruthless, robust and well armed men mingling together in the rendezvous.

Passing away the time in eating, drinking, card playing and an occasional hunt, they cautiously revealed a plot to raid an incoming supply train on the following Monday and asked the assistance of their new acquaintance. As it was then Friday, the time was short for Jack to formulate a definite plan of action. He must warn the soldiers at the fort in order that they could have a proper welcoming committee out when the bandits appeared. Since he was their latest recruit, he had to be on the alert constantly and not make a single false move for fear of arousing suspicion in the minds of the men.

Finally it occurred to him to suggest that he was going on a little hunt to relieve the monotony and to fetch back some fresh meat. This appeared to satisfy the few holding the hide-out while the others were here or there on various errands.

As soon as he was out of sight, Jack put spurs to his horse and sped toward the fort, by a circuitous route, one which only an experienced plainsman could have taken. Revealing the plot to the officers, he lost no time in getting back to the vicinity of the desperados' hide-out. The only time taken out on the return trip was to kill a nice young buck. Loading the game on his horse, he leisurely rode back to the robbers' stronghold.

Two or three of the gang were prone to question where the game came from, but Jack had little difficulty in disabusing their minds of any suspicions. After all he was tired and weary from the hunt, so he said, and at his suggestion, they quickly rounded up victuals and drink. Following the repast he lay down to rest, and to further formulate his plan of operation. There must be no slip-up, for these were desperate men who would stop at nothing to achieve their goal.

While he was mentally engaged with his plan, the fort was a beehive of activity. Acting upon Jack's suggestions, plans were being made to have a potent welcoming committee on hand to meet the desperados. One group was to proceed slightly beyond where the band was supposed to attack, the remainder to secrete themselves around the bluff where the robbers had attacked before—and where they had indicated to Jack they planned to repeat the raid.

Unsuspecting danger, the robber gang wound its way down to the place of attack. In a place of prominence, close to the leader, rode Jack. The soldiers had been briefed on how he would be dressed and were to watch for his signal. As the column rounded the bluff to their place of concealment, Jack's trained eye noted that the welcoming committee was on hand and in their proper place. Slowly he tilted his sombrero as if to scratch his head. At that movement of his hand, a volley of shots echoed from the bluff as the soldiers poured a deadly fire into the robber band. Reeling from this unsuspected reception, the band quickly dismounted, took cover and returned the fire. Desperados that they were, they were not easily unnerved by gunfire and did not intend to give up the rich prize of provisions, arms and ammunition they knew would be on the incoming supply train.

For several minutes the battle between the soldiers and the robbers continued in full intensity, even to hand-to-hand encounter. Jack himself was right in the thick of the fight. It is not known definitely, but there is every indication that

ROYAL HUNTING PARTY, 1872

From a photo by J. Lee Knight of Topeka, Kansas, and believed to be the only one taken of the distinguished group. *Left to right:* FRONT ROW–Gen. J. W. Forsyth, Lieut. Stordegraff, Col. M. V. Sheridan. MIDDLE ROW–Consul Bodisco, Chancellor W. T. Machen, Gen. Phil Sheridan, Grand Duke Alexis, Admiral Possiet, Gen. Geo. A. Custer. BACK ROW–Frank Thompson, Doctor Valdmir Kadrin, Col. Geo. A. Forsyth, Count Olsenfieff, Maj. Morris J. Asch, Col. N. B. Sweitzer, Lieut. Karl Tudor.

it was he who engaged the gang's chief in mortal combat.

Before long the superior numbers of the soldiers began to be felt. The sound of shooting had brought the other detachment back to the scene of the battle on the run. Almost as quickly as it had started the battle was over. The robber dead were buried and the wounded and prisoners were taken to the fort.

In telling of the incident years later, Jack's father, who followed earnestly the activities of his plainsman son, related that the government had paid Jack a handsome bonus for his skill and bravery in breaking up the gang and paving the way for the safe journey of the supply trains.

The year 1872 was a memorable one for Texas Jack. It was, without a doubt, the most remarkable of his varied career. Into it was crowded most of the activities which have assured him a permanent place in the annals of the West—scout, guide, Indian fighter, cowboy, hunter and actor.

First important event to start off the year had a decided tinge of international flavor. On January 13, 1872, the Grand Duke Alexis of Russia arrived in North Platte, Nebraska, for a buffalo hunt. Accompanied by his own staff and surrounded by a host of military dignitaries, the hunt was to be a remarkable occasion. General Phil Sheridan was host to the party which included, in addition to the Duke and his suite, such notables as: Lt. Col. James Forsyth, A.D.C.; Lt. Col. S. A. Forsyth, Military Secretary; Lt. Col. M. V. Sheridan, A.D.C.; Dr. M. I. Asch, Assistant Surgeon U.S.A.; Maj. N. B. Sweitzer, Second Cavalry; Gen. E.O.C. Ord.; Col. I. N. Palmer, Second Cavalry; Lt. Col. George A. Custer, Seventh Cavalry; Lieut. E. M. Hayes, Fifth Cavalry; and Capt. James Egan.

General Sheridan had previously made arrangements with his old scout, "Buffalo Bill" Cody, to act as guide for the party. He was also to scout out the land for good buffalo hunting and to make an agreement with Spotted Tail and his Indians to participate in the hunt and to put on a "show" for the distinguished visitors.

The *Omaha Weekly Herald* in its issue of January 17 con-

ROYAL BUFFALO HUNT, 1872

How an artist from *Frank Leslie's Illustrated Weekly* (Feb. 24, 1872) viewed the Royal Buffalo Hunt. The Grand Duke is shown in the act of killing his first buffalo.

tained nearly four columns devoted to the arrival of the Grand Duke Alexis and his party. A descriptive paragraph reads:

At 8 o'clock (January 13) the party left the train and took seats in ambulances. The Grand Duke, accompanied by Gen. Sheridan, rode in an open carriage, called a dray, drawn by four spirited horses. The Duke arrayed himself in an appropriate hunting suit with a short sword by his side, which costume set off his gigantic figure admirably. After entering the carriages, Buffalo Bill, in a buckskin suit, made his appearance on horseback and was presented to Alexis, and then in the capacity of guide to the hunting camp, led off . . . The permanent camp for the buffalo hunt is on Red Willow Creek, about fifty miles southwest of this post. . . . At 8 o'clock on the 14th, being the Duke's birthday, he mounted a gallant charger, properly armed and accoutred for the hunt, accompanied by Generals Sweitzer, Palmer, Forsyth and Custer, Lieutenants Hayes, Fowler, Clark, Stevens, Thomas and about twenty soldiers. They rode about seventeen miles before finding game, but here came upon a fine herd on a splendid hunting ground. The Grand Duke was anxious for the onslaught and was given the first hunt, which after a short chase resulted in his bringing down his first buffalo in splendid style, and proving himself a masterly horseman. The hunt resulted in killing between twenty and thirty buffalos.

Writing for Vol. X *Kansas Historical Collections* (1907-1908) James A. Hadley, an eye witness to the hunt, had this to say:

By daylight of the 14th the silvery notes of reveille roused the camp. Early as it was, great fires were blazing and the indomitable Custer had been long afoot. He had probably inspected, personally, every horse designed for a visitor, and scouts were scouring the country for the main herd. The hunters were duly ready for the field. They stood talking and laughing around the camp-fires, booted and spurred for the field, while in an outer circle drooped and nodded their respective mounts, ready saddled. The Muscovites were easily distinguished, their long fur coats in sharp contrast to the lighter wraps of the cavalry. General Custer announced the rules of the hunt. The whole party was to stop at a convenient distance from the game. The first attack was to be made by Alexis, accompanied by Custer, Buffalo Bill, and two Brulé warriors. An experienced buffalo-hunter was to ride beside and instruct each member of the prince's suite, the main party to remain in the background till Alexis made his first "kill," after which the hunt was to be free, and natives as well as foreigners were to bag as many as they could. Ambulances would follow the hunt in case of accidents.

The Grand Duke's hunting costume is described more in detail by a reporter of the *New York Herald* dated, "Camp Alexis, January 14, 1872."

The Grand Duke's hunting-dress was very appropriate and simple. It consisted of jacket and trousers of heavy grey cloth trimmed with green, the buttons bearing the imperial Russian Coat of Arms; he wore his boots outside his trousers; his hat was an Australian turban with cloth top. He carried a Russian hunting-knife and a Smith & Wesson revolver recently presented to him and bearing the coat of arms of the United States and of Russia on the handle.

Much has been written of the fine work done by the renowned Buffalo Bill as scout on the hunt, which is as it should be. However, what is not so generally known is, that the mild mannered scout upon whom Cody had come to rely so much at Fort McPherson and who had contributed so much to the success of the hunt in his quiet way, was none other

GEN. CUSTER AND THE GRAND DUKE
Gen. George A. Custer and the Grand Duke Alexis in hunting costume. From a photo taken in January, 1872, at the time of the Royal Buffalo Hunt.

Gertrude W. Crane

TEXAS JACK, Plainsman, 1872

Taken at the time he was a scout in western Nebraska this faded
but striking photo shows Texas Jack in the buckskin garb of a plainsman.

than Texas Jack. It was he whom Cody first called to guide the royal party as it started forth on its mission from North Platte. Buffalo Bill tells of it in his own words: [6] "When the whole party was mounted they started south, Texas Jack acting as guide until such time as I could overtake them." That his name should escape notice on this and other notable occasions is a tribute to his self-effacement and his desire to let others bask in the limelight.

A brief mention of the side arms carried by the two scouts may be of interest. Recently issued to various Cavalry units was the new Smith & Wesson American revolver of .44 caliber, sometimes referred to as Model 1869, or Model No. 3 American. There seems to be no question but that Buffalo Bill and Texas Jack were equipped with this latest type of revolver. Records of the Ordnance Department verify that quantities of these new arms were issued to units of the Third and Fifth Cavalries. Portions of the Fifth were still at the Fort at the time of the hunt.

For many years it was thought that Buffalo Bill was responsible for selling the Grand Duke on the merits of the new revolver and thus securing for its manufacturers a large order from the Russian government. This has been found to be erroneous since the Duke, as was mentioned above, was at the time carrying a presentation specimen of the same model, a gun which had been presented to him a month before by the officials of the Smith & Wesson factory—which factory, by the way, had been in production of the Russian order many months previous to the date of the hunt.[7]

Texas Jack's own gun, stamped U. S. on the barrel, is one of the nine hundred and ninety-six Smith & Wesson revolvers approved by Lt. Henry Metcalf of Army Ordnance on March 16, 1871, and issued during ensuing months to Cavalry units for the use of soldiers and civilian scouts in the field. The engraving, "TEXAS JACK COTTON WOOD

---

[6] *"Buffalo Bill's Life Story,"* published by Cosmopolitan Book Corporation, New York, 1920. pp. 230.

[7] See "Royal Buffalo Hunt" by the author in the *American Rifleman*, Oct. 1952.

SPRING 1872" unquestionably marks it as a presentation piece. It is believed that this nickel-plated, first model, cartridge revolver was presented to the scout in appreciation for some distinct service. One omission will be observed—the "s" is missing from the word "Springs" on the engraving. In view of the wording being slightly to the right, this could have been the fault of the engraver in not leaving sufficient space. However, older residents of the vicinity of Cottonwood Springs report that in the early days it was commonly referred to as Cottonwood Spring, due to there being only the one spring. Incidentally, when General W. H. Emory was in command at Ft. Cottonwood, he ordered the old cottonwood tree cut down. It seemed that some of the soldiers spent too much time in the shade of the old landmark. The spring has long since disappeared, but older residents today are able to point out to inquiring visitors the location of the once noted landmark.

Immediately following the royal buffalo hunt, elements of the Third Cavalry under the command of Col. J. J. Reynolds began replacing the Fifth Cavalry which had been stationed at Fort McPherson. Companies B, I and M, 3rd U. S. Cavalry arrived at the Fort on January 17th. The Field and Staff and Companies F & K did not arrive until March 12th.

The last detachment of the 5th U. S. Cavalry, which had started leaving on November 27, 1871, did not leave until January 31, 1872. These were under the command of Lieut. E. D. Thomas. Late in April a small marauding band of Indians raided McPherson station (now Maxwell) some five miles north of the Fort across the Platte River. Two or three men were killed and a considerable number of horses were stolen.

Co. B. 3rd U. S. Cavalry under the command of Capt. Charles Meinhold was ordered out to pursue and punish the Indians. Records of the War Department, quoting the returns from the 3rd Cavalry for 1872, has this to say of the engagement:

Co. B left Fort McPherson, Neb., April 25th in obedience to verbal orders of Post Commander in pursuit of a party of Indians who had stolen a number of horses the previous day. Followed the Indians 2 days and recaptured 2 of the stolen horses and killed 3 Indians on or near the Loupe River. Returned to post April 27, 1872. Distance marched 140 miles.

From this brief report it would appear the engagement was a very brief and minor one. In reality it seems to have escaped the notice of the newspapers in that vicinity at the time—after all, skirmishes with the Indians of that day were nothing unusual. That this particular encounter was above the ordinary is verified by the following statement of the adjutant-general of the United States Army:

On May 22, 1872, Mr. Cody was issued a Medal of Honor for gallantry in action at Platte River, Nebraska, the basis for the award being a report made by Captain Charles Meinhold, Troop B, 3rd U. S. Cavalry, dated at Ft. McPherson, Nebraska, April 27, 1872, descriptive of the pursuit of; and action with, a marauding party of Indians by a detachment of his company under his command.

This was the fight in which Cody received a minor scalp wound. And who was Buffalo Bill's assistant, and the one who was at his side rendering valiant service even to changing the tide of the brief battle? It was none other than Texas Jack, Cody's close friend and a scout at the fort. That others received the praise did not disturb this modest plainsman.

An examination of the records of the quartermaster general in the National Archives reveals that Texas Jack was hired as a guide under authority of Order No. 74 Hq. Fort McPherson. His rate of pay was $5.00 per day. Col. J. J. Reynolds 3rd U. S. Cavalry, was his commanding officer and 1st Lieut. John C. Thompson was acting Asst. Quartermaster at the time.[8]

According to the files of the 3rd Cavalry, activities were relatively quiet for some months after the above mentioned skirmish.

On April 18, 1872, Charles McDonald and his family

[8] National Archives and Records Service.

moved from the old home at Cottonwood Springs to North Platte. The son, W. H. McDonald, tells of a trip he and his father, together with a hired man, made back to the ranch in June to brand a herd of domestic cattle which had been left there.[9] At this particular time Texas Jack had very little to do, and he volunteered to help in the "round-up" job. Having had extraordinary experience with cattle, as well as being an expert with the lasso, his offer was readily accepted.

Several days were consumed in the branding and attending to other details around the ranch. All of their meals were taken at a boarding house run by Mrs. Jacob Snell on the post. At night they bunked down in the old store building. W. H. McDonald still chuckles as he recalls how he enjoyed those evenings with Texas Jack and the men folk. In the flickering lamp light they would get Jack to reminiscing of his days as a scout in the Confederacy and other amusing experiences of his earlier life. One particular story concerned his teaching experiences (probably in Florida). When he applied for a teaching job, one of the elder men on the school board asked which he taught—"Whether the earth is round or flat?" Quick as a flash Jack replied, "I can teach it either way you want it taught; I need the job."

In Mr. McDonald's opinion Texas Jack was not only the best story teller he remembers, but he was also one of the finest frontier scouts—and he met many of them in those early days around Cottonwood Springs, Fort McPherson and North Platte. He likes to tell of watching Jack, with boyish admiration, as he would remove the bridle from his horse and ride at a hard gallop right down the streets of North Platte. He thought Texas Jack was about the most skilled horseman he had ever seen, and the years have not changed his mind. He remembers that Texas Jack and Buffalo Bill were like two brothers; they were together so much during the time they were at Fort McPherson. Mrs. Cody's writings verify this close association of the two scouts.

During the summer, the Pawnees appealed to Generals

Sheridan and Ord for permission to hold a buffalo hunt. One reason for hunting in the warm weather was to enable them to dry their meat for winter storage. In giving their consent, both generals requested that two white men accompany the Indians on their hunt. General Sheridan, already familiar with Texas Jack's ability and qualifications, selected him as one of the leaders.

Often renegade white hunters would take advantage of the Indians while they were hunting—even to the extent of frightening away the herd just as the Indians were ready to make their kill. For the most part, the renegades were hide hunters, but their promiscuous firing often deprived the Indians of the quantity of meat they would have realized if they had been left to their own style of hunting. The white hide hunters were usually composed of the toughest element on the plains. To prevent any chance of trouble between the white hunters and the Indians was the reason the generals requested the presence of a white "trail agent," as they were called. In designating Texas Jack, Gen. Sheridan knew that the Indian's interest would be protected.

In some of his later writings, Capt. Luther N. North, who first became acquainted with Texas Jack on this hunt, estimated that there were about 4000 Pawnees and Omahas in the hunting party.[10] For traveling and carrying of supplies, between five and six thousand horses were used. Over five hundred tepees were required to house the Indians. The magnitude of the hunt gives an idea of the responsibility that rested upon the trail agent. The selection of Texas Jack for this difficult task was an indication of the high esteem in which his ability was held by the noted General and those in charge of Indian affairs for Nebraska.

A brief comment by the noted scout regarding the hunt is contained in the following letter to Buntline, which was published in the Nov. 18, 1872 issue of the *New York Weekly*.

---

[10] "*The Fighting Norths and Pawnee Scouts*" by Robert Bruce, Brooklyn Eagle Press, New York, 1932.

FRIEND NED:—I have just returned from one of the longest and hardest trips of my life across the plains. I have been in charge of three thousand Indians on their summer hunt. The game was very much scattered, consequently we had to go a great ways. I was three months away from the settlements. We met with a great many other parties of Indians, some war parties, some friends. Had some little fighting, but no general engagements. We killed some two or three thousand buffalo, packed our animals with dried meat, and reached the Indian Reserve some six days ago.

I shall be at leisure for the next six weeks. I wish you could contrive to pay us a visit during that time and go out on a hunt. Bill left here yesterday for a hunt in company with Judge Cronnes, of Omaha, and others. Will be gone several days. There is prospects of fresh war with the Sioux. Will be lots of chances for Indian pie before spring. I can take my tribe, the Pawnees, and clean them out two to one if the government will allow it. Will write more when I have leisure.

> Yours, as ever
> J. B. Omohundro (Texas Jack)

So well did the Pawnees respect the young scout that they referred to him as their "White Chief" and nicknamed him "Whirling Rope" in recognition of his skill with a lasso.

The hunt lasted from July 10 until September 14th, two months and five days, according to the statement Agent Jacob M. Troth sent in to the office of Superintendent of Indian Affairs in Omaha. Superintendent Barclay White's letter of transmittal to Washington is as follows:

> Omaha Neb., 9th mo., 19th, 1872

Respected friend:

I herewith enclose Agent Jacob M. Troth's certified voucher in duplicate, in favor of J. B. Omohundro, and amounting to $216.66 for accompanying and taking charge of the Pawnee Indians while on the summer hunt, in accordance with request of Gens. Sheridan & Ord, that a white man should accompany the tribe while out on the hunt.

Please remit draft for the above amount to the claimant at Ft. McPherson, Nebraska.

> Very Respectfully
> Thy Friend
> Barclay White
> Supt. Ind. Affairs

STATEMENT FOR TEXAS JACK'S EMPLOYMENT
AS TRAIL AGENT

Photostatic reproduction of the bill for Texas Jack's service as a trail agent with the Pawnees on their summer hunt in 1872.

to the
Hon. F. A. Walker
Commissioner
Washington, D. C.

Upon receiving the letter and bill for services, Mr. E. B. French, Second Auditor, directed the following reply:

October 7, 1872

Sir:

In reference to the claim of J. B. Omohundro for $216.66 for 2 1/6 months service in charge of the summer hunt of the Pawnee Indians in 1872, received from your office for settlement, on the 30th ultimo. I have to ask, that in view of the unusual character of the services for which pay is claimed, a copy of the "direction of Gens. Sheridan and Ord" be furnished to this office, that the same may be filed with the claim.

Very respectfully
E. B. French
Second Auditor

Hon. Commissioner
Indian Affairs

This brought forth a letter from H. R. Clum, Acting Commissioner, as follows:

Dept. Interior
Office Indian Affairs
Oct. 9, 1872

Hon. Second Auditor
of the Treasury
Sir:

I have received your letter of the 7th instant in which you ask to be furnished with "a copy of the direction of Generals Sheridan and Ord" referred to in the account in favor of J. B. Omohundro for services rendered while in charge of Pawnee Indians on the late summer hunt. Supt. White, in his letter transmitting said account to this office states that the services for which pay is claimed, were rendered "in accordance with the request of Generals Sheridan and Ord," which request it is presumed was a verbal one as no written directions on the subject accompanied the account.

The claim was allowed by this office on its own merits and on the recommendation of the Superintendent of Indian Affairs for the Northern Superintendency.

Very respectfully
Your Obt. Servt.
H. A. Clum
Acting Comm.

From all indications it would appear that governmental red tape is not something of recent origin. In answering a copy of the above letter, Superintendent White explains the claim in these words:

Omaha, Neb., 11 mo. 2nd, 1872

Respected Friend:

Previous to the Pawnees leaving their reservation for their last summer buffalo hunt, Agent Troth informed me that he had communicated directly with Gen'l Ord commanding the "Department of the Platte," and had received instructions from him and Gen'l Sheridan, directing him to place said Indians in the charge of two white men, while absent on said hunt.

He also recommended J. B. Omohundro as one suitable to such charge. After inquiry, I approved of the tribe leaving in the care of said Omohundro and Baptiste Bayhylle, a half blood, and U. S. Interpreter for the tribe. The former was to receive a stated compensation for his services. The latter receivd no pay for this special business.

A certified voucher in favor of J. B. Omohundro was forwarded to thee in my letter of 19th ultimo.

I have since received from Gen'l Ord a copy of a letter from the Second Auditor of the Treasury addressed to him, a copy of which I enclose, with a copy of Gen'l Ord's endorsement thereon.

Upon receipt of this letter I addressed Agent Troth, requesting copies of the letters of Gen'ls Sheridan and Ord mentioned above.

Copies of the letters forwarded to me are enclosed.

I would respectfully ask to be instructed as to the necessity of sending two white men with each tribe of Indians while absent from their reservations on Buffalo Hunts and if necessary, in what manner said white men are to be compensated for their services.

Very Respectfully
Thy Friend
Barclay White
Supt. Ind. Aff.

Hon. F. A. Walker
Com'd Ind. Aff.
Washington, D. C.

In transmitting the above papers to the Second Auditor Commissioner Walker indicates in the last line of his brief note dated Nov. 8, 1872, that he is a bit bored with all the red tape. He ends thus:

The said claim was allowed by this office and referred to you for settlement on the 26th, Sept. last.

Since no other correspondents is to be found, it is presumed that, after the delay occasioned by the above exchange of letters, Texas Jack received payment for his valued services.

Soon after this incident, the Earl of Dunraven, an English sportsman, together with Dr. G. H. Kingsley and a party of friends came out to Fort McPherson for a hunt. Buffalo Bill

Cody and Texas Jack were engaged as guides for the party. They had been out only a short time when Cody had a call to guide another party from Chicago—friends of General Sheridan and he felt he must do a favor for his friend, the General.

Since Cody was the better known, the Earl of Dunraven at first was a bit disgruntled at his leaving in the midst of a good hunt. It was not long, however, before Jack had completely won his respect and friendship by his outstanding ability. From then on, any time the Earl returned to America for a hunting trip, he would have no other guide but Texas Jack!

When the hunt with the Earl and his party was over, Texas Jack returned to Fort McPherson to find his friend, Buffalo Bill, in a quandary. It seemed that an earlier acquaintance of his, Col. E. Z. C. Judson, better known as Ned Buntline, a writer of dime novels, had been writing and urging him to come East and try his hand at acting. He felt the real Buffalo Bill, in person, would be a big drawing card. In fact while visiting in the East some months previously, Cody had been introduced to a theater audience and the response to the western scout had been terrific.

It is said that misery loves company and Buffalo Bill was in a predicament. Should he leave the life he knows and loves and venture out in a new experience? He sought Jack's advice and counsel, just as he had done on many occasions. Knowing that Buntline was also going to feature Texas Jack in some writings, Cody inquired if Jack would go with him. Always eager for any new adventure that offered a thrill, Jack's reply was, "Well, Bill, what are we waiting for?"

There being a lull at the time in buffalo hunting and scouting activities, the two scouts packed their suitcases and headed for Chicago, the footlights and fame. How they succeeded in their new venture—even beyond their fondest expectations—is related in the next chapter.

6

BUCKSKIN AND SATIN

WHEN the train carrying Texas Jack and
Buffalo Bill arrived in Chicago on Wednesday, December 11, 1872, Ned Buntline and a Mr. Milligan
were on hand to greet them. Only a few weeks before, Cody
had been the guide for Milligan and his party on a buffalo
hunt in western Nebraska. Now as a gesture of appreciation
the two scouts were to be his guests at the Sherman House
while in the city. After seeing them settled, Buntline was off
for a temperance lecture in one of the public buildings.

The next day the promoter took the two plainsmen over
to meet the manager of the Amphitheatre in which they
were to play. Jim Nixon, the manager, was highly enthused
with the appearance of the two western scouts. His enthusiasm quickly turned to dismay when it was discovered that
Buntline, in his excitement, had not even written the play—
let alone rounding up extras to take the part of Indians in
the show. It was then Thursday and the drama was to open
the following Monday evening. Nixon voiced his sentiments
in no uncertain terms. The contract must be cancelled!

At this the undaunted Buntline blithely asked the indig-
nant manager how much rent he wanted for the theater for
the next week. "Six hundred dollars" was the laconic reply.
"Gimme a receipt for half the money," shouted Buntline
as he slapped the money down on the table before the astonished Nixon. With the receipt in his pocket Buntline turned
to the scouts, who had stood silently by amidst all the con-
troversy between the two showmen, and said, "C'mon boys,
we've got work to do."

Back at the hotel the flamboyant Buntline was all action.
Sitting down at a table in his room, he began feverishly

"SCOUTS OF THE PRAIRIE," 1872

Ned Buntline   "Buffalo Bill"   "Texas Jack"
(E. Z. C. Judson)   (W. F. Cody)   (J. B. Omohundro)

This photograph by Gurney & Son of New York shows the three partners in the costumes they wore in the stage production of *The Scouts of the Prairie.*

to dash off page after page of script. Bellhops, clerks and others were called in to help copy the individual parts as he would complete a scene or act. Four hours later he burst in upon the astonished scouts with the news that the play was finished—and that the title would be, "The Scouts of the Prairie."

With a terse word to the boys to get busy learning their parts as they had a rehearsal coming up in the morning, Buntline grabbed his hat and took off to round up actors to take the part of Indians and lesser characters in the play.

Learning that the noted ballerina Mlle. Morlacchi was then in the city, Buntline sought her out. So vividly and enthusiastically did he describe his plans for the new western type of drama that he was successful in persuading her to join the troupe—at least for the opening performance.

Imagine if you can the situation in which Texas Jack and Buffalo Bill found themselves. Having never seen more than a few plays, let alone acting in one, their dilemma was one for which they would have gladly traded the charge of a band of hostile Indians. Having never flinched under frontier fire, they demonstrated the same courage in facing this new life. In this spirit they set about learning their parts. For the next two or three rehearsals the stage manager endeavored to coach the two would-be-actors upon the fine points of acting. Both admitted that it seemed an almost hopeless task—this business of learning to be actors overnight.

Sensing that the two scouts were terribly ill at ease and worried, Buntline took Buffalo Bill in hand for a bit of coaching in the art of acting. As a tutor for Texas Jack he could think of no better coach than Mlle. Morlacchi. Even though she was primarily a dancer, her long experience on the stage well fitted her for the task. And, a most enjoyable task it proved to be for the petite, dark eyed, dancing beauty with her satin slippers who thoroughly captivated the buckskin clad scout.

It was two extremely nervous scouts, dressed in fine buckskin, who gazed out from behind the curtain at the rapidly

Left: CHICAGO NEWSPAPER ADVERTISEMENTS, 1872
Reproduction of a three inch ad which appeared in the December 15,
1872 issue of the *Chicago Times*.
One column, one inch ad which appeared in the *Chicago Tribune*
under the date of December 15, 1872.

Right: SHOW BILL OF 1872-73
The Scouts of the Prairie used this type of show bill for their first
season.

NIBLO'S GARDEN,
LAST WEEK OF
THE SCOUTS OF THE PRAIRIE,
introducing the
ORIGINAL WESTERN HEROES,
BUFFALO BILL,   TEXAS JACK
NED BUNTLINE,
The peerless danseuse, Mlle. Morlacchi.
Twenty Indian Warriors,
THE SCOUTS OF THE PRAIRIE,
THE SCOUTS OF THE PRAIRIE.
Buffalo Bill, by the original hero ....Hon. W. F. Cody
Texas Jack, by the original hero...........J. B. Omohundro
Cale Durg..Ned Buntline
Dove Eye................................ ....Mlle. Morlacchi
SYNOPSIS—ACT I.
On the Plains—Trapper and the Scouts.
The Renegade's Camp—Peril of Hazel Eye.
Ned Buntline's Temperance Lecture.
Cale Durg at the Torture Post.
The Indian Dance—The Rescue.
ACT II.— Texas Jack and his Lasso.
The Loves of Buffalo Bill.
The Death of Cale Durg.
The Trapper's Last Shot.
ACT III.— The Scout's Oath of Vengeance.
The Scalp Dance—The Knife Fight.
The Triumph of the Scouts.
The Prairie on Fire.
The performance will commence with the roaring Farce
A KISS IN THE DARK.
MATINEES WEDNESDAYS AND SATURDAYS AT 2.

NIBLO'S GARDEN ADVERTISEMENT, 1872

Advertisement of *The Scouts of the Prairie*
during their appearance at Niblo's Garden, New
York, in March of 1873.

filling theater that opening night of December 16, 1872. It
was obvious that they were going to make their debut before
a "sell out" crowd. At last the footlights came on and the
curtain slowly arose on what was to be the beginning of the
most unique type of drama the American stage had ever
witnessed.

It took two or three repetitions of the cue before the two
plainsmen could get up enough courage to saunter out on
the stage. The applause which greeted them was tremendous;
it was indeed a splendid tribute to Texas Jack and Buffalo
Bill, the real heroes.

When the applause had ceased and it was time to proceed
with the play, the great theater was strangely silent—both
scouts were utterly speechless. "Where have you been,
Buffalo Bill?" inquired Buntline, as Cale Durg in the play.
His eyes catching sight of his friend Milligan sitting in a box
close to the stage, the only reply to enter Cody's head was,
"Why—why I've been out hunting with Milligan." It so
happened that Milligan was a very popular person in Chicago

and this bit of "off the cuff" repartee made a big hit with the audience. And to the credit of the audience it should be pointed out that they were not there to see fine drama interpreted by skilled actors; they had come to see Texas Jack and Buffalo Bill, of whom they had heard so much. What mattered if they faltered in their lines, or if their acting lacked the polish of the trained actors? They were seeing the real heroes in person, from the Old West, and they were enjoying it to the fullest.

Author's Collection

SOUVENIR PHOTO OF "THE SCOUTS OF THE PRAIRIE", 1872
Every lady attending the première showing of *The Scouts of the Prairie* was presented with a small photograph of the four leading actors—Ned Buntline, Buffalo Bill, Mlle. Morlacchi and Texas Jack.

The following cast of characters, together with a synopsis of scenes and incidents of the show is taken from an old Boston Theatre program:

THE RAY
Boston, Wednesday, March 5, 1873
BOSTON THEATRE
J. H. Booth, Lessee and Manager

THE SCOUTS OF THE PRAIRIE!

ENGAGEMENT LIMITED TO SIX NIGHTS AND TWO
MATINEES!

THIS AFTERNOON

The Entertainment will commence with a Beautiful Terpsichorean Comedietta, written by Colonel Judson, to introduce the Graceful MORLACCHI in Four Exquisite Dances, entitled

LOVE'S BATTLE!
Or, Fairy Transformations!

MINETTE, with Entrance Sortita, Spanish Bolera, Caprice Schottice and Polish Mazurka ....M'LLE MORLACCHI
CAPT. EURORE ....HARRY WENTWORTH
FIFTEENTH AMENDMENT ..GEORGE C. DAVENPORT
MADAME DUBOIS ....ELLA BEACH

To conclude with Ned Buntline's Sensational Drama of

SCOUTS OF THE PRAIRIE

BUFFALO BILL (by the original hero) ..HON. W. F. CODY
TEXAS JACK (by the original hero) ..J. B. OMOHUNDRO
CALE DURG ....NED BUNTLINE
MORMON BEN ....HARRY WENTWORTH
PHELIM O'LAUGHERTY .....GEORGE C. DAVENPORT
CARL PRETZEL ....WALTER FLETCHER
HAZEL EYE ....SENORITA ELOE CARFANO

INDIANS

WOLF SLAYER (specially engaged for this part) W. J. FLEMING
BIG EAGLE ....JOS. J. WINTER
LITTLE BEAR ....GEO. B. BEACH

Pawnee Indian Chiefs

AR-FI-A-KA ....GRASSY CHIEF
AS-GE-TES ....PRAIRIE DOG
AS-SIN-AN-WA ....WATER CHIEF
TE-CO-TIG-POWN ....BIG ELK
KIT-KOT-TONS ....GREAT RIVER
CHUK-KAK ....SEVEN STARS
DOVE EYE ....M'LLE MORLACCHI
NATOLAH ....MRS. BEACH

MATINEE ON SATURDAY AT 2 O'CLOCK!
Friday, Benefit of BUFFALO BILL and TEXAS JACK. Saturday
Night Farewell and Benefit of NED BUNTLINE

THE SCOUTS OF THE PRAIRIE
SYNOPSIS OF SCENES AND INCIDENTS

ACT 1—Scene 1.—On the plains, Cale Durg, the Trapper. Arrival of Buffalo Bill and Texas Jack. Story of the Hunt. A warning from Dove Eye. Danger. "We'll wipe the red skins out." On the trail. The war-whoop.

Scene 2.—The Renegade's Camp. Mormon Ben. Phelim O'Laugherty and Pretzel. O'Laugherty's continued drouth. Danger to Hazel Eye.

Scene 3.—Hazel Eye's poetic tribute to Cale Durg. Hazel Eye surprised. Cale Durg to the rescue. The Renegade foiled. Wolf Slayer, the treacherous Ute. Cale Durg overpowered. Search for the bottle. Cale Durg's temperance rhapsody.

Scene 4.—Doomed to the torture-post. Dove Eye's appeal to the Chief. "Death to the Pale Face." Then burn, ye cursed dogs, burn. The blazing fagots. Dove Eye's knife. The severed bonds. Cale Durg defiant. "We'll fight ye all." Timely arrival. Buffalo Bill and Texas Jack. "Death to the Redskins." Rescue of Durg.

ACT II—Scene 1.—Mormon Ben, Pretzel and Phelim O'Laugerty. O'Laugherty declares he is not a Mormon. The meeting with Indians. What Mormon Ben wanted. What O'Laugherty wanted. Wolf Slayer's disdain of fire water. "It's the curse of the Red Man as well as the White." The departure of the Indians for the war-path. Dove Eye's invocation to the Great Spirit.

Scene 2.—Dove Eye and Hazel Eye, the two friends. Buffalo Bill declares his love. It is reciprocated. Texas Jack arrives and interrupts the meeting. "The Indians are coming." Buffalo Bill and Texas Jack retire to ambush. How Jack ropes them in. "Buffalo Bill." "That's the kind of man I am." How they scalp them on the plains.

Scene 3.—Phelim O'Laugherty in "The Shakes." Cale Durg to the rescue. God's beverage. Love scene between Texas Jack and Hazel Eye.

Scene 4.—The search for Hazel Eye. "The cage is here, but the bird has flown." The trail. The search and capture of the Forest Maidens. Dove Eye's contempt for the Renegades. Cale Durg arrives upon the scene. "Fly, fly, your enemies are too many." Cale Durg never runs. The capture and death of Cale Durg. The Dying Curse. The Trapper's Last Shot.

ACT III—Scene 1.—Dove Eye and Hazel Eye. Grief for Cale Durg. Buffalo Bill and Texas Jack. Bill's oath of vengeance. "I'll

not leave a Red Skin to skim the Prairie." Dove Eye dejected.
The White Girl and Red Maiden's affections. "We'll be sisters."
Revenge for the Slain Trapper. Vengeance or Death.
Scene 2.—The German Trader. The loss of the bottle. Carl
Pretzel's Agony.
Scene 3.—The Scalp Dance. Eagle and Wolf Slayer. "I come
to kill you." The Knife Fight. Death of Wolf Slayer. Dove Eye's
glorious revenge.
Scene 4.—Carl Pretzel and Mormon Ben on their last legs. No
prospect for the fiftieth wife.
Scene 5.—Dove Eye's faith in the Manitou. The Indians. Buffalo
Bill's red hot reception. "Give it to them, boys." One hundred
reds for one Cale Durg. The American Scout triumphant. Great
Heavens, the PRAIRIE ON FIRE!

The play itself was a highly melodramatic presentation
of life on the frontier—Indians, renegade whites, beautiful
maidens and, of course, the scouts. Highlights were the fights
in which Texas Jack and Buffalo Bill "wiped out" the Indians in every act or so. The theater was permeated with the
aroma of burning powder as the two popular scouts blazed
away at the redskins with blank cartridges in their six-guns.

The Chicago audience was seeing the earliest use of the
lasso in a dramatic production as Texas Jack roped the rebellious savages. It was he who first introduced a roping act
on the American stage.[1]

One feature of the show which contributed immeasurably
to its success was the specialty dancing acts by the beautiful
and graceful M'lle Morlacchi, whom Buntline had also engaged for the heroine's part in the drama. The story of this
winsome beauty from Italy will be told in another chapter.
suffice to say here that observing eyes, even at that time,
might have detected a more than casual glance in her direction by the handsome Texas Jack.

Even though neither of the scouts recited the correct lines
in their script during the entire first performance, it was
obvious that here was a hit play—so well was it being received by the audience. Immediately following the first

---

[1] *The Herald Democrat* (Leadville, Col.), Sept. 8, 1908.

TEXAS JACK IN COSTUME, 1872

Texas Jack as he appeared in Buntline's drama *The Scouts of the Prairie* at its première showing in Chicago on December 16, 1872.

night's opening, plans were rushed for going on the road with the show. Every performance saw enthusiastic crowds filling the theater for the unusual entertainment. The week's run in Chicago proved a financially profitable one—so much

PORTRAIT OF Mlle. MORLACCHI IN THE ROLE OF
AN INDIAN MAIDEN

A striking pose of the charming Mlle. Morlacchi taken in 1873 by the noted Gurney & Son Studio in New York.

so that the manager of the Amphitheatre expressed a desire to join the troupe as a partner.

Shortly after the curtain was lowered on the final performance, the entire troupe entrained for St Louis, the first "stop" in their new tour, a tour which was to popularize this western type of drama and in turn add to the notoriety of Texas Jack and Buffalo Bill.

The embarking upon a theatrical career called also for an entirely new life for the two enterprising scouts. No longer did they bunk down in open tents or sleep on the prairie under the stars; now they were to be confined to tiny dressing rooms and stuffy hotel bedrooms. No longer could they whistle for a trusted saddle horse to come a running to carry them to their destination. Henceforth, they were to ride the dusty seats of swaying and creaking railway coaches. Truly it was a new experience for these pals of the plains.

Shortly after the show opened in St. Louis, Ned Buntline was arrested on a twenty year old charge of having jumped bail. Texas Jack and Buffalo Bill, also included in the warrant, were hustled off to jail along with Buntline. The bombastic promoter was all but ready to start shooting up the place when Texas Jack quieted him with this bit of wisdom. "If we were back on the plains we might have something to say, but here in the city it's no use. We must take what comes."[2] After a bit of fanfare, the charges were dropped and the trio released. The whole thing apparently was a cleverly devised scheme hatched out in the fertile brain of Buntline to gain added publicity for the show.

Col. Homer W. Wheeler (Fifth Cavalry U. S. Army) in his book *The Frontier Trail* tells of this incident concerning the two scouts at the time their show was playing in St. Louis:[3]

In 1872 I spent the holidays in St. Louis. At that time Cody and "Texas Jack" Omohundro were playing in Ned Buntline's (Colonel Judson) drama entitled, *The Scouts of the Prairie.* Linggard's Company in New York was also there; also *The English Blondes.* All were stopping at the Southern Hotel.

One evening after the play we went out for some refresh-

[2] *The Great Rascal* by Jay Monaghan, Little, Brown & Co. New York, 1952.

[3] Published by the Times-Mirror *Press,* Los Angeles, 1924. Used by special permission.

DOVE EYE, 1872

The talented and nationally known, Mlle. Morlacchi as "Dove Eye" in the western drama, *The Scouts of the Prairie*. A native of Italy she found real enjoyment in portraying Indian maidens in dramas of the Old West.

ments. An actor named Hudson of Linggard's Company accompanied the party. Of course, we went into one of the fashionable resorts. Cody had a way of knotting his hair under his hat so that people would not recognize him. Hudson was wearing Texas Jack's sombrero, and passing himself off as Texas Jack.

An elderly gentleman who had been imbibing rather freely joined our party. He addressed most of his conversation to Hudson, under the impression that he was talking to Texas Jack. He told him that he admired him very much, but that he did not have much use for Buffalo Bill. This, of course, caused us much amusement. Presently, he took from his finger a very nice old-fashioned seal ring and gave it to Hudson as a token of friendship.

A day or so later one of the hotel employees asked me if I was connected with *The Scouts of the Prairie* company. I told him no, that Cody and I were old friends on the plains, and while in the city I was passing quite a little time with him. The clerk then stated that there was a prominent man and his family living at the hotel, a man who, at times, drank too much; that he had been out a few nights before, and while in his cups had given away a valuable ring; that he had had it for a number of years and was very anxious to get it back. The gentleman had an indistinct idea that he had given the ring to one of the members of *The Scouts of the Prairie* company.

I told the clerk that I knew all about the transaction and would be pleased to assist in recovering the ring. I went to Cody about it, and he said that of course the ring must be returned and that he would see Hudson and get it. He went to Hudson and told him the ring must be given up. Hudson replied that he had given it to his sister in the presence of the ladies of the other troupes, and that under the circumstances he dislike to ask her for it. This young lady was called "Laughing Eyes" by Cody and Texas Jack. She was indeed a very attractive person. In the meantime, I had been introduced to the gentleman who had given the ring to Hudson. He told me he was willing to get the young lady another ring. I replied that I did not think Cody would permit that, although neither he nor Texas Jack had anything to do with the transaction.

To shorten the story: We got the ring back and the man gave me an order on Jackard's jewelry store for a ring to cost not more than one hundred dollars. I bought a very pretty ring for less than one-half the amount.

One evening, after the play and refreshments, Laughing Eyes was presented with the ring before quite a number of the show people. In the next morning's *Globe-Democrat* was published an article to the effect that Buffalo Bill and Texas Jack had presented the young lady with a very valuable diamond ring. The gentleman appreciated my services and before I left the city he gave me and some of my friends a very nice dinner.

Following their successful appearance at St. Louis, the troupe left for Cincinnati—and the East. That their new western type of drama was making a tremendous hit is best evidence by the newspaper reviews of the cities visited. Every place it was the same story of huge, cheering and enthusiastic audiences. Indeed *The Scouts of the Prairie* was blazing a new trail in the annals of the stage—one that was marked by such comments as these few scattered specimens taken chronologically from their first season:

CINCINNATI . . . Pike's Opera House . . . Dec. 30, 1872
   The sidewalk and the entrance last evening at Pike's gave evidence of a startling sensation. A dense crowd collected about the ticket office and stretched out on the sidewalk on both sides of the door. Suppressed Indian yells in the crowd told of the nature of the sensation. It was *The Scouts of the Prairie* announced to be given that caused such a commotion. . . . The play is beyond all precedent in the annals of stage lore. . . . It has in it all the thrilling romance, treachery, love, revenge, and hate of a dozen of the richest dime novels ever written. . . . Buntline as *Cale Durg; W.* F. Cody as *Buffalo Bill* and *Texas Jack* are the leading characters. . . . Morlacchi was as graceful as ever. . . . The play bids fair to have a most wonderful run, for its novelty is so striking, and its subject is such a popular one with so many readers of thrilling border tales, that the temptation to see the real actors in those tragedies can not be resisted. . . .
                              (*Cincinnati Daily Gazette*, Dec. 31, 1872)

ROCHESTER . . . Corinthian Hall . . . Jan. 31-Feb. 1, 1873
   Ned Buntline's sensational drama, *Scouts of the Prairie*, was given in Corinthian Hall last evening before a packed audience. The original heroes "Buffalo Bill," Hon. W. F. Cody, and "Texas Jack," J. B. Omohundro, with the celebrated novel writer, Col. E. Z. C. Judson, "Ned Buntline," appeared in the prominent parts of the drama, and judging from the frequent and prolonged applause, gave the best satisfaction. The above celebrities were, of course, the great attraction, yet the "Peerless Morlacchi," Dove Eye, and the redskin chiefs had plenty of admirers. The

scouts rendered their part in that bold, free and easy manner, characteristic of frontiersmen, representing their characters "to the life."

(Rochester Express)

ALBANY . . . Martin Opera House . . . Opened Feb. 5, 1873
  The Scouts of the Prairie was produced last evening before a crowded house. The hall rang with the warwhoop of the Pawnee and the crack of hunters' and scouts'˜ rifles for over two hours. Somebody was shot, scalped or in some manner killed in most every scene.

(Albany Argus Feb. 6, 1873)

BOSTON . . . Boston Theater . . . Opened March 3, 1873
  Buffalo Bill and Texas Jack, real prairie guides, and their Pawnee aides, lend an intensity to the piece that has never been witnessed in representations of the semi-savage drama here before, and their efforts were well appreciated. Not only did the galleries applaud the actors, but the novelty of the style of greeting awakened the enthusiasm of the parquet in sympathy. Indeed, with the occupants of the high-priced seats, it was difficult to determine wherein they were most gratified, whether with the performance on the stage or the quaint expressions of the youngsters in the upper tier. M'lle Morlacchi made up well as an Indian maid, and her dancing in the introductory sketch "Love's Battle," was much admired. Those who delight in sensations of the most exciting order will not fail to see the distinguished visitors from the western plains before they leave.

(Boston Evening Transcript March 4 ,1873)

  A somewhat novel entertainment is provided at this theater (Boston Theater) this week, and one which, judging from last night's experience, is likely to bring out the masses in strong force. It is in the form of a sensational drama entitled, *The Scouts of the Prairie*, which introduces the veritable heroes of the plains, Buffalo Bill and Texas Jack. . . . In addition . . . M'lle Morlacchi, the favorite danseuse, appeared in a speaking character. . . . The play of itself is an extraordinary production with more wild Indians, scalping knives and gun powder to the square inch than any drama ever before heard of. . . . The chief interest, however, settles in the performance of the Hon. W. F. Cody (Buffalo Bill) and Mr. J. B. Omohundro (Texas Jack). Two finer specimens of manly strength and beauty were never seen on the stage or off the stage. They have not a great amount of acting to do, the most liberal part of their duties consisting of "cleaning out" redskins. . . . M'lle Morlacchi acquitted herself with great credit both as an actress and a danseuse.

(*Boston Journal*, March 4, 1872)

The patrons of the Boston Theatre were treated to a decided sensation last evening in the production of Ned Buntline's drama of *Scouts of the Prairie*. Although the weather was quite stormy and the traveling bad, a very large audience assembled and, with the exception of the parquette, all parts of the theatre were filled, so that a great many were compelled to stand. Those who occupied the upper portion of the house were hardly of the class that usually frequents this place of amusement, and were rather inclined to be boisterous. The entertainment began with a terpischorean comedietta called "Love's Battle," . . . to introduce M'lle Morlacchi in several beautiful dances . . . many of M'lle Morlacchi's friends were present and honored her beautiful and artistic dancing and poses with deserved applause . . . and when a few minutes later *Buffalo Bill* and *Texas Jack* made their appearance there was a perfect yell of delight. . . . In fact so much pleased were the "gallery gods" with these two personages that it was somewhat difficult for others in the cast to receive even respectable treatment. . . . *Buffalo Bill* (Hon. Wm. F. Cody) is a noble, good looking and very powerful man. . . . *Texas Jack* (Mr. J. B. Omohundro) is somewhat younger, a man also of excellent physique, and although not so heavy as Buffalo Bill, is evidently a person of great physical power. . . . All, however, were vigorous in their encounters with the redskins, and used the knife and revolver in a manner that rather astonished the audience. The Indian mode of warfare, their hideous dances, the method they adopt to "raise the hair" of their antagonists, following the trail, etc., or the way their enemies deal with them, manner of throwing the lasso, &c., are forcibly exhibited, and this portion of the entertainment alone is worth the price of admission.

(*Boston Traveler*, March 6, 1873)

NEW YORK . . . . Niblo's Garden . . . . March 31, 1873 . . . The representation was attended by torrents of what seemed thoroughly spontaneous applause; and that whatever close criticism may detect; there is a certain flavor of realism and of nationality about the play well calculated to gratify a general audience.

The Indians, as well as the scouts, are the genuine article. . . . Hon. William F. Cody, otherwise "Buffalo Bill," occa-

LEFT: NIBLO'S GARDEN POSTER, 1873
Reproduction of a large theatrical poster advertising the show during its New York appearance at Niblo's Garden.

RIGHT: ROCHESTER NEWSPAPER ADVERTISEMENT, 1874
Newspaper advertisement from the *Rochester Daily Union and Advertiser* of March 10, 1874, featuring Buffalo Bill, Texas Jack and Wild Bill in *The Scouts of the Plains*.

sionally called by the refined people of the eastern cities, "Bison William," is a good-looking fellow, tall and straight as an arrow, but ridiculous as an actor. Texas Jack is not quite so good looking, not so tall, not so straight, and not so ridiculous.

(*New York Herald*)

PHILADELPHIA . Arch Street Theatre. Opened April 21, 1873
Buffalo Bill and *Texas Jack* are the right men in the right place at the right time all through the drama. If a man is to be saved from the redskins, these men do it. If other acts of a like humane and daring character are required of them, they respond in a ready, off-hand manner, which is truly captivating to those who are fond of high-spiced dramatic food. In this way *Buffalo Bill* and *Texas Jack* are introduced to the audience. They are both fine specimens of the men of the frontier and the prairies. *Buffalo Bill* is a tall, straight, athletic man, in the prime of life, with a light, springy tread, and an open, honest face. He looks able and willing to do many of the deeds in earnest which are represented on the stage. . . . *Texas Jack* is a fit companion for Buffalo Bill in physical attributes, and they fill the stage to the exclusion of all others from equal notice and consideration. . . . M'lle Morlacchi personates *Dove Eye*, and adds her attractions to those of the heroes of the piece.

(*The Age*, April 22, 1873)

RICHMOND . . Richmond Theatre . . Opened May 12, 1873
"Ned Buntline" has written a red-hot blood and thunder play called *The Scouts of the Prairie*, and on Monday night next he, assisted by Buffalo Bill, Texas Jack, Cale Durg and ten wild Pawnee Indians, will enact this thrilling drama at the Richmond Theatre to the mingled horror, wonder and delight of all who can get in. A strong force of police will be on hand, and the first Regiment will be under arms nearby to suppress any tendency on the part of the wild Injins to scalp the audience. Here is a sensation that all can appreciate and enjoy, and it will run for four nights only. The question is not, "Who will go?" but rather "Who *can* stay away?"

(*Richmond Wig*, May 7, 1873)

The house was packed from top to bottom, and the play which was good of its kind, was received with the wildest applause . . . and the audience went home well pleased with what has been the best thing in the sensational way that has ever visited us."

(*Richmond Wig*, May 13, 1873)

The theatre was crowded again last night. . . . The applause testified to everybody's delight, and all who miss seeing and hearing this company will have to regret having missed one of the most striking and stirring dramas of the age, performed by men who have gone through in stern reality what they simulate upon the stage.

(*Richmond Wig*, May 14, 1873)

Ned Buntline and his two confreres, Cody and Omohundro, better known as "Buffalo Bill" and "Texas Jack," with their "Live Indians," drew another good house. . . . The audience again exhibited their delight over the sham combats, war dances and daring rescues of Indian Maidenhood in distress. . . . The way the Scouts handle their navy revolvers takes the "boys," and is the main secret of their success. Were it not, however, for the handsome appearance made by these two gentlemen, and that they represent in a measure real scenes of which they have been the actual heroes, and having bonafide Indians on the stage, the performance would be tame and unprofitable, indeed.

(*Richmond Enquirer*, May 15, 1873)

One interesting feature of the troupe's visit to Richmond was the three day visit of Texas Jack's family to the city as special guests of their famous son and brother. A family reunion was held at the Exchange Hotel. Mr. M. H. Omohundro, only living brother of Texas Jack, still has a vivid memory of that visit with the older brother whom he idolized.[4] Jack had gifts for all of the family. Still prized by his younger brother is a peculiar pocket knife and an attractive ring which Jack had presented to his step-mother.

NORFOLK . . . . Opera House . . . . Opened May 16, 1873

Buffalo Bill, Texas Jack, Ned Buntline and their "Ingins" filled the Opera House last night with one of the largest audiences ever assembled within its walls. . . . The crowning piece of the night, that which excited the juveniles to the wildest demonstrations of delight, was Ned Buntline's famous blood and thunder drama of, *The Scouts of the Prairie*. . . . Whenever Texas Jack and Buffalo Bill (both fine looking fellows) appeared on the stage, the audience cheered and applauded lustily. . . .

(*Norfolk Journal*, May 17, 1873)

---

[4] Correspondence with Malvern H. Omohundro.

Buffalo Bill and Texas Jack are fine looking men, and have that certain daredevil look and manner that we have always been led to attribute to the western hunters and scouts. The performance was in every way worthy of the fame and the gentlemen who conduct it.

(Norfolk Journal, May 18, 1873)

After a brief stop in Harrisburg, Penna., the troupe wound up its first season at Port Jervis, N. Y., on June 16, 1873. The season had proved to be a most successful one, financially and otherwise; but, both of the two main characters were somewhat disappointed that their share of the profits did not amount to more. They felt that Buntline had taken advantage of them and remonstrated with him for it, but to no avail. The selfish attitude of Buntline was to prove his undoing, for the two scouts who had been his main attractions parted company with him and went on their own way to fame while Buntline's star began a rapid decline.

Had it not been for the steadying influence of Texas Jack upon Buffalo Bill during that first season, it is doubtful whether or not Cody would have kept on in the show business. It seems to be the consensus of students of history around North Platte, Cody's old home, that to Texas Jack should go a major share of the credit for Buffalo Bill's continuing on the stage. They base this belief on the fact that many times during the first year Cody was ready to throw the whole business of acting overboard, but was persuaded otherwise by his friend, Texas Jack, who was enjoying this new experience and who seemed to have had a leveling control upon the noted scout.

After a several weeks' hunting trip in western Nebraska, during which they served as guides for a Mr. Scott (Chicago hatter), Eugene Overton and Elisha Green (a son-in-law of Remington),[5] the two scouts, invigorated by their sojourn in the great out-of-doors and the life they loved so well, again turned eastward.

In the Rochester (NY) Daily Union and Advertiser for August 20, 1873, there appeared this significant note:

---

[5] Charles R. Nordin, *Nebraska History Magazine*, Oct.-Dec., 1927.

THREE SCOUTS OF THE OLD WEST, 1873

"Wild Bill"	"Texas Jack"	"Buffalo Bill"
(J. B. Hickok)	(J. B. Omohundro)	(W. F. Cody)

According to John M. Burke this photograph of the three scouts, and pards, was taken at Syracuse, N. Y. sometime during their theatrical tour together.

"Texas Jack," of frontier notoriety, has been in the city a few days on a visit to friends. He left for New York this morning where he will join "Buffalo Bill." The two have dissolved partnership with Ned Buntline and are organizing a new dramatic company. "Texas Jack" says his sympathies are with the Pawnees in their fight with the Sioux, and hopes the government will interfere in behalf of the Pawnees, as they are the best "Injuns" and inferior in numbers to the Sioux.

One of the greatest services Buntline rendered to Texas Jack and Buffalo Bill was bringing them together with Major John M. Burke. The genial and resourceful Major Burke idolized the two scouts. Thus, it was but a small matter to persuade him to throw his lot in with the new combination when the two approached him with their idea. Burke's background had been that of actor, manager, critic and city editor on various small papers. He had a pleasant personality which made him very popular in newspaper, railway and theatrical offices. Tribute has been paid to Major Burke as being the greatest press agent of the show business, both in this country and abroad.

In organizing their new company, Buffalo Bill and Texas Jack immediately thought of their old friend, J. B. "Wild Bill" Hickok, whose name was a byword in the Old West.

"TEXAS JACK"

"BUFFALO BILL"

"WILD BILL"

AUTOGRAPHS OF THE THREE SCOUTS

It was their reasoning that with Wild Bill in the troupe they would have a drawing card par excellence. A bit reticent at first, Wild Bill nevertheless did accept their invitation to join them in the new enterprise.

At this time Texas Jack was engaged in a new venture. Leaving his old friends, Buffalo Bill and Major Burke, to work out the details of the show, he hied himself back to Rochester for a very special purpose as this note from the *Rochester Daily Union and Advertiser* of September 1, 1873, will indicate.

Matrimonial—John B. Omohundro (Texas Jack), of scout notoriety was yesterday joined in the bonds of matrimony by Rev. Father Stewart to M'lle Morlacchi, the celebrated danseuse. The happy pair subsequently held a reception at the Osburn House and in the evening took cars for Buffalo, where Madame Omohundro plays an engagement this week.

Further details of this happy event will be recorded in a subsequent chapter. It should be noted here, however, that Mlle. Morlacchi had her own theatrical troupe and when not on a tour with Buffalo Bill and Texas Jack, she carried on under her own name.

Fred G. Maeder's thrilling drama of western life, *The Scouts of the Plains*, was selected as the play for their second season's tour. Cast of characters included:

BUFFALO BILL . . . . .W. F. Cody
TEXAS JACK . . . . .J. B. Omohundro
WILD BILL . . . . .J. B. Hickok
PALE DOVE (wife of Texas Jack) . . . . .Mlle. Morlacchi
JIM DAWS, a renegade horse thief . . . . .Frank Mordaunt
AUNT ANNIE CARTER . . . . .Miss Jennie Fisher
ELLA . . . . .Miss Lizzie Safford
UNCLE HENRY CARTER,
        a friend of the scouts . . . . .J. V. Arlington
NICK BLUNDER, with song and dance . . . . . .Walter Fletcher
TOM DOGGETT, in cahoots with Daws . . . . . .W. S. McEvoy
EBENEZER LONGLAND,
        Government Peace Commissioner . . . . .A. Johnson
TALL OAK, a Kiowa, but on the square . . . . .W. A. Reid
BIG THUNDER, a Comanche Chief . . . . .B. Meredith

BEAR CLAW, a Comanche brave ....H. Mainhall
RAVEN FEATHER ....J. W. Buck

The 1873-74 season was but a continuation of the astonishing success engendered by their tour of the previous year.
While Wild Bill was with the show, the tour was not without
its amusing incidents. At Titusville, Penna., (Parshal Opera
House Nov. 6, 1873) word reached the scouts that a group
of "roughs" were on a spree and had boasted how they were
going to clean out Buffalo Bill and his pals. At the request
of the hotel manager the show people entered the theater from
a private side door which adjoined the hotel. Wild Bill was
anxious to see just what kind of a bunch it was that wanted
to clean up on them, so unbeknown to the rest he sauntered
down to their hangout in the billiard room. The result is best
described by Buffalo Bill in his earliest autobiography.[6]

. . . as he stepped into the room, one of the bruisers put his
hand on his shoulder and said: "Hello, Buffalo Bill! We have
been looking for you all day."

"My name is not Buffalo Bill; you are mistaken in the man,"
was the reply.

"You are a liar!" said the bruiser.

Bill instantly knocked him down, and then seizing a chair
he laid out four or five of the crowd and drove the rest out of
the room. All this was done in a minute or two, and by the
time I got downstairs, Bill was coming out of the bar-room
whistling a lively tune.

"Well!" he said, "I have been interviewing that party who
wanted to clean us out."

"I thought you promised to come into the Opera House by
the private entrance?"

"I did try to follow that trail, but I got lost among the canons,
and then I ran in among the hostiles,' said he, "but it's all right
now. They won't bother us any more. I guess those fellows
have found us." And sure enough they had. We heard no
more of them after that.

While the troupe was at Portland, Maine, (Music Hall
January 29-30, 1873) Wild Bill had considerable difficulty
getting to sleep, due to continual talking and commotion

---

[6] Frank E. Bliss in "*The Life of Hon. William F. Cody*, known as
Buffalo Bill."

in an adjoining room. In exasperation he finally got up, dressed and went to the room to see what was going on. There, he was surprised to find some of the business men of the city whom he had met the day before. They were having a friendly hand of poker and invited him to sit in the game. Bill allowed that as long as they wouldn't let him sleep he guessed it would be all right, provided they would post him a bit on the game, as he wasn't very familiar with it. Bill purposely made a lot of blunders and asked a lot of irrevelant questions at first to fool the others. But a few hours later with several hundred dollars in his pockets, he arose to bid his new friends adieu with this piece of advice. "Adios m' friends; better think twice after this before waking a man up and inviting him to play poker."

This brief note from the *Portland* (Maine) *Advertiser* of January 30, 1874, is an indication that the drawing power of the scouts had not diminished.

Scouts of the Plains. We can only say today that Wild Bill, Buffalo Bill, Texas Jack and Morlacchi drew an immense audience to Music Hall last evening. The applause was frequent and hearty and Morlacchi's dancing aroused immense enthusiasm.

In Albany (N. Y.) the following paragraph announced the coming of the troupe, for a three day stand:

At Martin Opera House, Thursday night, there will be "lifting of hair" and all the other concomitants of border life. The realistic drama of the *Scouts of the Plains* will be given to salute their olfactories with its "savory" odor. Buffalo Bill, Texas Jack and Wild Bill, with blood in their eyes, and pistols loaded with blank cartridges, will crack away at the treacherous Redman, whole poor Lo will reciprocate, but will, in the drama as in dime novels, finally succumb. Morlacchi will dance and sing, and fun, powder, blood, hair, etc. will be promiscuously mixed in one conglomerate mass.

(*Albany Argus*, Tues. Feb. 24, 1874)

This same paper had this terse comment three days later: . . . The performance concluded with the realistic drama entitled *The Scouts of the Plains*. A commendable improvement is noticed in the action of the border heroes, Buffalo Bill, Texas Jack and Wild Bill. The performance on the whole is a good one, and is

FIVE FRONTIER SCOUTS

From an old tintype made at Denver, Colorado in the early seventies. From left to right: Elisha Green (son-in-law of Eliphalet Remington the gun manufacturer), Wild Bill Hickok, Buffalo Bill Cody, Texas Jack Omohundro and Eugene Overton (a New York restaurant man).

really worth seeing by those who are interested in that style of drama. . . .

Because of his pranks Wild Bill had developed into a problem for Buffalo Bill and Texas Jack. One of his favorite pastimes had to do with "killing" the Indians in the sham battles. In this connection he took a keen delight in discharging his pistol close enough to their legs to cause them to cry out in pain from the powder burns. Time and time again Wild Bill promised to stop his fun, but every now and then he would break over.

When the company reached Rochester, Buffalo Bill was particularly anxious that everything would go off as smoothly as possible. This was now his "home town" (he had moved his family there a few months previously) and he wanted the show to make a good impression on the citizens.

That the troupe lived up to their reputation is verified by these two paragraphs from *The Rochester Daily Union and Advertiser*:

The Opera House was never before filled with a more dense crowd than that assembled to witness the performance last evening. The entertainment was no doubt satisfying to those who witnessed it, but in as much as the writer could not get a glimpse of the stage; all criticism in regard to the setting of "Buffalo Bill," "Texas Jack," "Wild Bill," and Morlacchi will be omitted. It is not probable that even an ordinary earthquake could keep away the crowd that will assemble tonight when the *Scouts of the Plains* will be produced for the last time. (March 11, 1874)

Every foot of space in the Opera House was occupied last night on the occasion of the second and last appearance of the *Scouts of the Plains*. There is no doubt that "Buffalo Bill" and his followers would draw crowded houses here were they to remain two weeks at least, but we are willing that this should not be, as there are people in Lockport, Buffalo and Erie who are dramatically famished for a sight of "The Scouts" and who having seen them will lead better lives ever afterwards. Thinking of this we are resigned. (March 12, 1874)

During the second act of the play on their last performance in Rochester, Wild Bill could restrain himself no longer—

he must have his fun of singeing the Indians' legs. As the curtain fell, the Indians threatened to quit unless Buffalo Bill and Texas Jack would see to it that they were not molested any more. Their patience at an end, and in exasperation, they told Wild Bill that he would have to quit the foolishness or leave the show.

Wild Bill merely stared at his friends for a moment, turned and made for his dressing room without any comment. At the close of the next act the stage carpenter hunted up the scouts and said, "That long-haired pal of yours, who left in a huff a few minutes ago told me to tell you that you could take your damned old show and go to thunder!"

After the performance was over that evening Buffalo Bill and Texas Jack went out to look up their old friend. They found him at the Osburn House in good humor again, his anger having cooled off quickly. They tried to persuade him to finish out the season with them, but his mind was made up to go back to the plains. He had not had "too much hankerin' for this show business anyway" and now was as good a chance as any to pull out. To him "play-acting was only making a fool of one's self."

Even though they hated to see him go, both scouts inwardly could not find it in their hearts to blame him. There was a certain freedom on the prairies not to be found on the stage. Against that kind of competition the two actors had little to offer.

As they shook hands and bade Wild Bill farewell it was once again the three scouts of the Old West talking—"pards for life." This was without doubt the last time the three were ever together. Two years later Wild Bill was shot in the back at Deadwood, S. C., by the cowardly Jack McCall! When asked why he did not walk up to Wild Bill and shoot him like a man, McCall replied, "You don't think I wanted to commit suicide, do you?"

Much has been written concerning Wild Bill's leaving his two friends in the show business. Hidden away in the files of a Rochester newspaper of that date is this intensely enlightening interview with one of the paper's reporters. It is reprinted here for the first time, exactly as it appeared in the columns of the *Rochester Democrat and Chronicle* under the date of March 13, 1874:

WILD BILL

He Leaves Troupe for the Western Frontier—The Way His Friends Treated Him

Having seen the stalwart form of Wild Bill (J. B. Hickok) passing down State street yesterday afternoon, and knowing that the troupe of scouts with which he has been appearing upon the stage for some time past had departed for Lockport where they performed last night, we ventured to approach the hero and enquire the reason why he tarried behind his fellows. Our hand was grasped with considerable warmth in his which appeared to be an iron vice from which we were glad to be released. After devoting a few words not at all complimentary, to the blustering March winds that were whirling the snow through the streets, he began to relate why he was not with the troupe, and we should have had the whole matter explained then and there, had not an impudent youngster crying *"Union* or *"Express"* come down the street with the loud cry of, "Oh! stag his nibs wid the long hair!" Now it is well known that Bill wears his hair in the flowing style prevalent on the frontier; and this, together with the tall form and manly deportment of the man, attracted the attention of the newsboy and caused him to give vent to several exclamations of no particular importance to the student of polite literature, but very well calculated to draw the attention of everyone within the sound of his voice to us. Bill was not at all affected by this strange proceeding. He remarked that he had witnessed it in hundreds of towns, so often, in fact, that it was an old thing to him. We suggested, however, that we should move along, to which he willingly consented. The few staring mouth-opened children of the pave who had gathered were soon left behind, and as we passed into Exchange place, there was but one left, and he took to his heels because Wild Bill stopped and looked at him. We were then informed that Bill had received a call to the frontier. Recognized as one of the best scouts and Indian fighters that have appeared upon the great western frontier, his services are highly valued and eagerly sought for when there is danger of war with the Red man. Just now there is considerable commotion at Fort Laramie and some of the Indian agencies, especially the Red Cloud and Spotted Tail agencies. The Sioux has been seen in his war paint and General Sheridan thinks he may begin his attempt to seek the paleface in a few weeks. At this time and amid such scenes as these, the services of Wild Bill will be invaluable to the United States troops. It is this, together with a longing desire to return to the free, wild life he loves so well that has called our hero away. He will first proceed to New York where he has some business to transact, remain there a few days and then go direct to the frontier. Buffalo Bill, Texas Jack, and the other scouts did not like to have him leave, but when he said he must go, the noble-hearted fellows presented him with $500 apiece, and each gave him a splendid revolver, bidding him to make good use of it among the "Reds." He had nothing but kind words to speak of the boys, as he familiarly termed the other scouts. He wished them all manner of good fortune and was sure they would receive it. Wild Bill is a noble fellow, a true-hearted child of nature, one of those men which one occasionally comes in contact with and ever after retains a place in his memory. We shook hands with the hero, bade him good-bye, and wished him a pleasant journey to his far western home. He left at 12:15 this morning for New York.

During the first part of May, 1874, the troupe played in Milwaukee, Wisconsin. Soon after this they wound up their second tour—one which had further added to their laurels and finances.

During the 1874-75 season Texas Jack was absent from the combination. He had taken leave to guide the Earl of Dunraven on an extended hunting trip, which is enlarged upon in a later chapter.

Little is known of the next season together. Buffalo Bill's Autobiography has only this brief mention of it. "For the season of 1875-76 Texas Jack and I reorganized our old combination and made a very successful tour."

From all available material it would appear that this was the last season these two great scouts toured together. From then on there are but fragmentary accounts of their theatrical days.

Part of the time Texas Jack traveled with his wife, Mlle. Morlacchi and her troupe, and at other times she traveled with him and his show.

In May of 1877 the Texas Jack combination played in St. Louis. Advance press notices included the following:

On Monday Texas Jack, the simon-pure Omohundro, with Donald McKay and his band of Redskins will sound the war-whoop and indulge in a general scene of scalping after the manner of Sitting Bull and Captain Jack. Texas Jack has improved wonderfully since he first appeared in this city, and as the scenes he enacts are taken from real life in the Black Hills, the boys ought to be satisfied.

(*St. Louis Globe Democrat*, May 6, 1877)

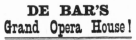

DE BAR'S
Grand Opera House!
FIVE NIGHTS ONLY, Commencing
Tuesday Ev'g, May 8th.
MATINEE—SATURDAY
The Real
TEXAS JACK!
(J. B. OMOHUNDRO.)
THE GREAT CHIEF AND SCOUT
Donald McKay
AND HIS
WARM SPRING INDIANS!
THE PEERLESS
MORLACCHI,
Miss Maude Oswald,
And a full Dramatic Company, in the great Border Drama
TEXAS JACK
IN THE
BLACK HILLS!
FRIDAY EVENING, MAY 11, BENEFIT OF
TEXAS JACK
Prior to his departure for the Plains.
Globe-Democrat Job Print.

Brown Bros., photo

DE BAR'S OPERA HOUSE
HANDBILL, 1877
Handbills such as this were distributed in St. Louis at the time Texas Jack and his troupe appeared there on May 8, 1877.

TEXAS JACK, 1877
Texas Jack in the stage costume he wore while heading his own show troupe in 1877.

A week later the same paper had this to say of the performances:

Texas Jack and his band of redskins are gaining . . . in public favor, but do not draw as full houses as they deserve. They have a show that is altogether unique—a live horse that equals Mazeppa—a whole band of Indians from the Modoc lava beds: a French squaw, an Italian dancing girl, three or four mountain hunters and trappers, and Texas Jack, who is a whole team of himself. Of course a combination of this kind cannot be expected to do as finished acting as the Fifth Avenue Company, or the Boucicault Troupe, but they enact some very thrilling scenes, and give a fair sample of life on the border, where the irrepressible conflict of races goes on as in the old pioneer days. (May 12, 1877)

Considerable has been written on how Maj. Burke was an inseparable companion of Buffalo Bill. What is not so generally known is that he also was tremendously fond of Texas Jack and his wife, Mlle. Morlacchi, and that he often traveled with them in their combinations. Maj. Burke was a part of the Texas Jack show when it played in St. Louis. The St. Louis Globe Democrat of May 12, 1877, has this to say concerning the noted press agent who often went by his stage name of "Arizona John":

"Arizona John," whose other name is Burke, is a member of the Texas Jack Combination, which nightly demonstrates in a realistic drama the ability of a pale face to sweep from the face of the earth whole platoons of the "pesky red varmits"! In all of Texas Jack's retinue there is no one who can annihilate whole tribes of Indians with greater facility than "Arizona John." Armed with a revolver filled with blank cartridges, he kills six of the "red demons" at a single fire.

Then in à la dime novel fashion is attached the following lurid paragraph:

A sample instance of A. J.'s matchless bravery in fighting the red men while on the frontier, is told by an admiring friend. A. J. had started on a tramp of 2000 miles through a hostile Indian country. One afternoon, while cautiously treading the wilderness, he came across nine stalwart bucks in their war paint and armed to the teeth. They were seated upon a log, faces all to

TEXAS JACK

EARLY LITHOGRAPHIC SKETCH OF TEXAS JACK IN A
STRIKING POSE

the east, chewing tobacco. Arizona approached stealthily. He placed the long steel ramrod of his trusty rifle in the barrel. He took aim carefully and fired. The ramrod did its work well. It passed through the noses of the nine braves. Arizona approached and taking hold of the center of the ramrod, led the party of prisoners to the nearest fort.

From all indications Texas Jack and his troupe were performing during the season of 1877-78, though it is not possible to name the many places and dates of showing. In February, 1878, they appeared in New York. *The New York Herald* in its issue of February 19, 1878, gives the following review:

THE OLYMPIC–TEXAS JACK

The arrival of the Texas Jack Combination at the Olympic appears to have attracted all the boys in New York, as last night the capacious galleries of that theatre were packed to suffocation, and the gallant Jack from Texas received a royal greeting when he made his first appearance. The performance commenced with the comedy of *Thrice Married*, in which M'lle Morlacchi exhibits a versatility that very few actresses can boast of. She appears in four characters—a French costumer, a Spanish danseuse, a French singer, and a midshipman. She was rather unfortunate last night, as a vile orchestra made singing almost an imposibility, but her voice seems to have strengthened since she was last in the city. *The Scouts of the Plains* followed the comedy, and when Texas Jack made his appearance there was a terrific round af applause, which was repeated throughout the evening after every round of musketry. At the close of the first act, the Emerald Zouaves of Jersey City, commanded by Captain Gill, assisted in the slaughter of the unfortunate redskins, and the enthusiasm up stairs was perfectly terrific. Between the acts Jack was called out and presented with a rifle by some gun manufacturers, which he accepted with a few words of thanks. The piece ran very smoothly and is likely to prove a big attraction for the Olympic.

Very little is heard of Texas Jack during the next two years; it is presumed that he spent at least a part of his time hunting, a sport which he so thoroughly enjoyed. Some time was undoubtedly spent on the stage, and last, but not least by any means, much time was enjoyed in the comfortable home he and his attractive wife occupied in Billerica, near Lowell, Massachusetts.[7]

From the files of the *Rocky Mountain News*, Denver, Colorado, under the date of March 16, 1880, comes this brief review indicating that Texas Jack was still on the stage:

TEXAS JACK'S APPEARANCE

The Adelphia was crowded to its utmost capacity last evening by enthusiastic admirers of Texas Jack, who made his first appearance in his border drama entitled, *The Trapper's Daughter.* With the exception that the company were not thoroughly up in their parts, the first appearance of the Texan was a decided success and won hearty applause from the audience.

From Denver, Texas Jack moved on to Leadville, which at that time was the boom town of the West. First account of his appearance there is recorded as March 25, 1880, at which time he was playing at one of the theatres on Chestnut Street. A month later the Grand Central Theatre announced the following attraction in a large front page display advertisement in the daily paper: "Commencing Sunday Evening April 25, The Genuine Original BLACK CROOK! . . . with M'lle. Morlacchi and her Grand Ballet Troupe."

With the Leadville performances the curtain was lowered on the theatrical days of Texas Jack and Mlle. Morlacchi—troupers in buckskin and satin.

[7] *Lowell Daily Citizen*, (Lowell, Mass.), July 24, 1886.

7

MLLE. MORLACCHI—
Première Danseuse

No SAGA of Texas Jack would be complete without giving considerable attention to the petite and charming bit of feminity who was his wife and companion for the last few years of his adventurous life.

Fortunately enough information has been preserved on this celebrated stage personality to provide a fairly accurate account of her life. Those contemporary sources will be drawn upon most heavily for this brief biographical sketch.[1]

Guiseppina (Josephine) Morlacchi, daughter of Anthony and Mary Morlacchi of Milan, Italy, was born in 1846. When she was but six years of age, her parents placed her in a school at LaScala. Here she remained for a period of six years, during which time special attention was given to perfecting her in the art of dancing. Her debut was at Carlo Felice Theatre in Genoa in 1856. Following her graduation from the Academy, she again visited Genoa and Naples, and in 1862 journeyed to London. In a comparatively short time she became an outstanding dancer, even appearing at Her Majesty's Theatre. On a trip to the Continent in 1864 she visited Florence, Turin, Lisbon and other noted cities. At Lisbon she was invited by an imperial order to dance at the Royal Theatre at Barcelona, Spain.

It was during her visit to Lisbon that she became acquainted with John DePol, the noted artist and manager. Late in the fall of 1867 she was persuaded by DePol to return with him to America where she was to play in the DePol Parisian Ballet. This company was brought into being as a counter

---

[1] *Rochester Democrat and Chronicle*, Sept. 1, 1873.
Lowell Daily Citizen, July 24, 1886.
New York World, Aug. 1, 1886.

Mlle. MORLACCHI

A daring photographic study of this celebrated ballerina who introduced the Cancan to the American stage.

attraction to Jarrell & Palmer's "Black Crook," which at that time was showing at Niblo's Garden.

Mlle. Morlacchi became an immense attraction following her American debut in the spectacle of the "The Devil's Auction," on Oct. 23, 1867 at Banvard's Museum located at 1221 Broadway in New York City. This popular playhouse, of which DePol was manager, was later known as Daly's Theatre.

One writer in describing her arrival in New York tells how the orchestra of the theatre serenaded her with Strauss waltzes and operatic airs, beneath the windows of her suite in a Fifth Avenue Hotel. Recognizing the tremendous publicity value of his welcoming stunt, Manager DePol insured her legs for $100,000, whereupon a sporting paper commented, "Mlle. Morlacchi is more valuable than Kentucky (one of the finest race horses of that day).

A critic of the New York Tribune wrote of her extraordinary debut in these glowing words: "Mlle. Morlacchi is a beautiful creature, and she came upon the stage like a sudden ray of light. She is of the spiritual order of woman, small, delicate, fiery, with a fine little head and a luminous face, and she dances with all her soul as well as with all her body."

Following her triumphant debut, it was a succession of appearances in the eastern theatres. Opening on Dec. 3rd at the Academy of Music, New York, the show enjoyed two weeks run before it took to the road.

Gratified at the spontaneous reception accorded his show in New York, DePol moved with his company to Boston. On the evening of Dec. 23, 1867, *"The Devil's Auction"* featuring Mmes. Morlacchi, Blasina and Diani as the chief dancers, opened at Whitman's Continental Theatre.

On January 6, 1868, the DePol Company was billed at the Theatre Comique, and with this billing there came into being a new type of dance for the American stage. It was announced on a playbill of that date that the performance would close that night with the . . .

"Grand Gallop (sic) Cancan, composed and danced by Mlles. Morlacchi, Blasina, Diani, Ricci, Baretta and Kruger; accom-

Mlle. MORLACCHI IN "THE DEVIL'S AUCTION"

Mlle. Morlacchi's American debut was in *The Devil's Auction* at Banvard's Museum, New York, November, 1867. It is said by a prominent
writer of the time that the gifted Italian actress was its chief attraction.

panied with cymbals and triangles by the coryphees and corps
de ballet."

Over a half century later Dock Square, an eye witness,
writing in the Boston Herald (Nov. 12, 1911) recalls quite
vividly this first introduction of the cancan to an American
audience. He wrote as follows:

Every one was surprised, no one could understand the meaning
of the queer name, but after the opening night all doubts were
removed; no ladies applied for tickets after that; but the male
sex crowded the theatre to the point of suffocation. Whether
acquainted or not, everyone was asking, "Have you seen the
cancan?" . . . So intensely became the fervor of the nightly
throngs that some wag spread the rumor that the Barnicoat
Engine Company (steamer No. 4) had orders to be on hand
to quell the excessive heat of the auditors by streams of cold
water!

Boston Public Library

THE MORLACCHI BALLET

As to the production, everything was strange, particularly the
music. The curtain went up showing a stage crowded with
Amazonian warriors garbed in ancient Roman costumes—swords,
spears, shields and brazen helmets. Then came the marching and
manoeuvres, when suddenly as both warlike bodies fell back,
right and left, the music changed to a wild and fierce measure,
the Amazons clashing their swords on the shields in time to
the tune, when, in dashed, one at a time until there were ten, the
most astonishing dancers that Boston had ever seen. They
twisted, crossed, turned and spun, unwinding as they did,
unmeasurable yards of muslin until they stood, were it not for

silk tights, apparently *"in puris naturalibus."* Each dancer kept on a military head-dress to the last. The 10 were divided into two sections, the first being captained by Mlle. Morlacchi, the second by Mlle. Diani. Morlacchi's squad was brunette, Diani's was blonde, the yellow tresses of the latter waving wildly as they whirled around.

The reception accorded the new dance must have been most enthusiastic because accounts record that the company was still playing at the theatre in the latter part of February.

On Nov. 9, 1868, the play *"Lurline"* opened at the Theatre Comique. The hand-bill announcing the show carried this significant comment at the end: "The original Morlacchi cancan." Added was this note about the cancan.

Gaiete—G Mazzeri, Albertine
Abandon—L Mazzeri, Penzera
Vivicito—Morlacchi, Baretta

Dancers listed included: Louise and Giovannia Mazzeri, Leopoidina Baretta, Albertine Duchateau, Zameri Panzera and La Petite Augustine.

Advertisements in the daily papers concerning the show spoke in glowing terms of the "Great Morlacchi whose power of thoughtful, fanciful dancing—music addressed to the eye —has never been equaled by any artist who has visited this country." They went on to add that: "They confidently anticipate a renewal of the furor of excitement among the most cultivated classes of our citizens."

Even the decorous *Evening Transcript* in its theatrical review column made the comment, "the concluding rollick of the cancan which will never grow tedious . . ."

In December, 1868, she returned to the Continental, which then had been rechristened the Olympic and was under the managership of J. B. Booth. She appeared in the *Seven Dwarfs* at the Boston Theatre in August, 1869. Later, in November to be exact, she played in the spectacular *Mid-Summer Night's Dream* at the Selwyn's Theatre and later the Globe.

In 1871 she filled two engagements at the Boston Theatre, the first in June, and the second in November and December, at which time she was assisted by the Majilton Family of grotesque dancers. The new cast opened November 27 in *The French Spy* which ran for the greater part of two weeks. Their next show was interrupted by a gala event with a tinge of international flavor. The Grand Duke Alexis of Russia, while on a tour of America, visited Boston on Friday, December 8th. The enthusiastic welcome given by the citizens culminated in a grand ball given in the evening in the Boston Theatre. The auditorium was re-floored for dancing and the entire interior of the theatre was lavishly decorated. It was an occasion that lingered long in the memory of the city. Since the noted Morlacchi, premier ballerina of the stage was then showing at the theatre, it goes without saying that her talents were used to the fullest in preparing an outstanding entertainment program for the visiting Royalty. The following Monday, Mlle. Morlacchi and her troupe, in combination with the Majiltons, opened in the play, *The Wizard Skiff*.

On December 16, 1872, she was billed as a feature attraction in Ned Buntline's western drama, *The Scouts of the Prairie* with Buffalo Bill and Texas Jack, a show which was then opening in Chicago. So well was she received that she continued with the show for the entire season. Her specialty dance numbers were received with unbounded enthusiasm everywhere the company appeared.

To some it might have seemed that this skilled and refined young actress was throwing away her talents by appearing in the then new and unproven type of "Wild West" drama. Indeed, the contrast between the subtle charm and grace of the old world type of dancing and acting to this flamboyant and boisterous type of western melodrama must have been terrific.

The name of Mlle. Morlacchi, première danseuse, was well known to patrons of the theatre, for she had at that time been a popular American stage personality for over five years. It was not strange then that Buntline should engage this noted dancer as one of the feature attractions, along with the two noted scouts, for he well knew of the drawing ability of her name among theatre goers.

BOSTON THEATRE

J. B. BOOTH . . . . LESSEE AND MANAGER.

Friday Evening, Sept. 10, 1860.

BENEFIT OF MR. ROBERT BUTLER.

The Gorgeous Oriental Pantomime, founded on a series of Siamese Tales, replete with Tricks, Changes, and Transformations, entitled the

SEVEN DWARFS;

Or, Harlequin and the World of Wonders.

The Cast of the Pantomime will embrace the following Artists engaged expressly for it:

ROBERT BUTLER,

THE INIMITABLE AMERICAN CLOWN.

Mr. J. SANDFORD, as HARLEQUIN.
Mr. CHARLES ORISIDE as PANTALOON.
Master MARTIN as SPRITE.
Miss LILLIE WHITING as COLUMBINE.

WITH 150 AUXILIARIES.

The Manager has also the honor to announce having effected an engagement with the justly celebrated

MORLACCHI TROUPE,

LED BY THE GREAT

M'LLE GUISEPPINA MORLACCHI.

| GIOVANNA MAZZERI. | LOUISA MAZZERI. | Mll'e ADRIAN. |
| M'lle CORRIDINA. | M'lle EVERS. | M'lle CATANIA. |

Forming the best Ballet Troupe now in Boston.

CHARACTERS IN THE OPENING.

MATALSKOFF, the Seer of the Burning Mountain		Mr J. Hagan
STARGAZE		Mr. McClorkey
MOONSTRUCK		Mr. Gledhill
PLANETALL		Mr. Robertson
METEOR	Seven Wise Astrologers of the East	Mr. Davidson
VENUSBOUND		Mr. Ware
LUMINARY		Mr. Hasting
ECLIPSALL		Mr. Markwell
MOULAUGH, the Enchanter of Evil		Mr. H. Weaver
PING SING, his faithful Slave		Mr. J. Taylor
CASHDASM		Mr. Wallace
CASHDASH	The Seven Dwarfs,	Mr. Smithson
CASHDASH		Mr. Hartwell
CASHLASH	Brothers of the Burning Mountain	Mr. Wilson
CASHPASH	Sorcerers, under the control	Mr. Patson
CASHPASH	of Moulaugh.	Mr. Willis
CASHPASH		Mr. Watson
PRINCE COLIQUORE, Rightful Heir to the Throne of Siam		Mr. JAS. SANFORD
CASHCASH, a Double-Distilled Spirit		Mr. ROBERT BUTLER
CASHLASH, his First Cousin		Mr. J. Collins
TOREYPUGMAGNANIMOUS, Emperor of Siam		Mr. Chink
CHAPULTITOOGOWELL, his Grand Vizier		Mr. Martin
OROKO		Mr. Wakeley
MOROKO		Mr. Mose
FOROKO	Six Powerful Golden Demons, Allies	Mr. Hook
JOROKO	of Moulaugh.	Mr. Simons
LOROKO		Mr. Samis
BOROKO		Mr. Weis
MAGOG		Mr. Davis
BOROGMME		Mr. Johnson
THISTLE		Mr. Sawyer
LECHINA	Seven Learned Giants	Mr. Marsh
ATHENTE		Mr. Mario
NAPOLIANA		Mr. E. Smith
DESERTALE		Mr. W. Johns
PURE SPIRIT, a powerful Fairy		Miss H. Tracy
PRINCESS FLORIZADO, transformed into a White Swan		Miss LILLIE WHITING

Dancing Fairies, Spirits of Evil, Spirits of Good, etc., etc., by a powerful Corps de Ballet.

FOR SYNOPSIS SEE PRECEDING PAGE.

New York Public Library

A page from a theatrical program of the Boston Theatre announcing the Morlacchi Troupe.

Mlle. MORLACCHI, Danseuse

This album portrait shows the noted actress in a daring stage costume of the time.

That the young ballerina could foresee possibilities in the new Western type drama and lend her support for its success, is indicative of her mature thinking. The years have proven the wisdom of her action. In the eighty years that have passed since that December night in Chicago when the western scouts and Indians met in mortal combat on the stage of the amphitheatre, "westerns" have never lost their thrill. They seem to have a peculiar and popular appeal for Americans in all walks of life.

If Mlle. Morlacchi had contributed nothing more than this to the theatre, her place among stage personalities would be secure. But, she had already won a permanent place in stage annals by her ability, charm and captivating personality, attributes which were not to diminish during the too few years left to her.

Of course, there was another reason for Mlle. Morlacchi's desire to be with *The Scouts of the Prairie*. This reason was a tall, dark haired, handsome scout by the name of Texas Jack. During the months the company was on the road, they were frequently seen in each other's company, strolling down the street or dining together before or after the show. It did not take a lot of deduction to see that here was a couple of young people with more than casual interest in each other.

With the picturesque western scout and the demure première danseuse, it was love at first sight and a genuine affection for each other. Many times before, others had vied for the attention of this darling of the American stage. At one time while she was playing at the Grand Opera House in New York, the notorious and wealthy Jim Fisk slipped a diamond ring on her finger as she was waiting for her cue to go on the stage. When the act was over, she sent for him and handed the ring back to him. "Oh, it's real!" said Fisk, adding, "Oh, bother! You know it's of the first water and worth $5,000." "Bah!" said Morlacchi, with a shrug, "I can earn that with one of my toes."

It is no secret that the rotund Maj. Burke was also a suitor. In fact, he once observed that he had met but one god and a goddess in his life. The god, of course, was Buffalo Bill, to whom he gave the most loyal service for some forty-four years of his life. The goddess was Mlle. Morlacchi. But against the youthful Lochinvar from the prairies, the press agent could offer but feeble competition.

At the close of the 1872-73 season for *The Scouts of the Prairie,* while Texas Jack was on a hunting trip with Buffalo Bill, Mlle. Morlacchi resumed her appearances upon the stage with her own troupe for the summer months.

While filling an engagement in Rochester, N. Y., in August, 1873, she received a visit from Texas Jack, who was then on his way to meet Buffalo Bill, the purpose of which was the organizing of their own show for the coming season.

Their conversation must have included other topics than —well the weather for instance—because ten days later Texas Jack was back in town. The result of this visit is best told in a story which appeared in the September 1st issue of the *Rochester Democrat and Chronicle*:

THE BRAVE AND THE FAIR

Marriage of Madamoiselle Guiseppotta Morlacchi and "Texas Jack"—The Ceremony Performed Yesterday at St. Mary's Church in this City.

Last winter fortune decreed that the charming and famous danseuse, Mlle. Morlacchi, and John B. Omohundro, known throughout the country as "Texas Jack," should meet in the city of Chicago. It proved to be a case of love at first sight. The fair actress immediately took a liking to the gallant scout of the prairies, the renowned Indian fighter and buffalo hunter. The affection ripened, until it took the form of a declaration of love on the part of Mr. Omohundro, which resulted yesterday in a ceremony which made the twain one. Our citizens who have been delighted for the past fortnight with the graceful acting of M'lle Morlacchi need no description of her personal appearance. For the benefit of outsiders, however, we may say that she is a native of Italy, and was born in Milan, about twenty-five years ago. Like most of her countrywomen, she is a brunette, whose personal beauty is heightened by a grace of manner that is unsurpassed. She is a highly educated lady and such as have been fortunate enough to gain her personal acquaintance are loud in

Mlle. MORLACCHI IN MILITARY COSTUME

A splendid example of an early lithographic drawing for the cover of a theatre program is this one featuring the Morlacchi Ballet Troupe.

their praises of her accomplishments and character. The man of her choice is a magnificent specimen of physical manhood. He is about six feet in height and of the finest proportions. A native of Virginia, born in 1846, the blood of Powhatan flows in his veins, and the acquiline nose, jet black hair, erect form, and piercing eye of that famed warrior are reproduced in the gallant "Texas Jack." He arrived in this city Saturday from New York and took rooms at the Osburn House. It was rumored during the day that he came on business of importance—indeed nothing less than his marriage to M'lle Morlacchi. A reporter of the *Democrat and Chronicle* called on the gentleman to learn the facts. Mr. Omohundro with great courtesy stated that M'lle Morlacchi and himself were to be united in the holy bonds, but when, he was unable to state, although he believed the event would take place very soon. The fact was that the lady, who is a rigid Catholic, insisted that the ceremony should take place under the forms of that church and the gallant groom acquiesced willingly. He had been brought up in that faith himself but during his life on the plains, remote from all churches and religious ministration, he was, perforce, compelled to forego some of the duties incumbent on all members of the church. This fact occasioned some delay, but suffice it without going into further details, that all obstacles were removed and yesterday morning the marriage took place in St. Mary's Church. With a proper contempt for vulgar display which is too often made on such occasions, the interested parties desired that the ceremony be performed with as much privacy as possible. Their wishes were complied with. Immediately after the 8 o'clock Mass, which the affianced pair attended, and after the congregation had departed, Father Stewart appeared behind the altar rail and in a short time the vows were plighted and words were spoken which united two hearts that beat as one. Mr. and Mrs. William McCarthy appeared as groomsman and bridesmaid, and with a few personal friends of the contracting parties were the only witnesses. After leaving the church the newly wedded pair were driven to the Osburn House where they received the congratulations of their friends and remained until yesterday afternoon when they left for the West, carrying with them the best wishes of a host of friends for a long life and conjugal happiness.

M'lle Morlacchi has an engagement to play at Buffalo this week, which we understand will conclude her performances on the stage for the present at least. She has been highly successful in her profession and we are informed that she owns a farm near

Mlle. GUISEPPINA MORLACCHI

The wife of Texas Jack was the beautiful Mlle. Guiseppina (Josephine)
Morlacchi of Italy, . . . première danseuse of the American stage,
during the late sixties and seventies.

New York worth not less than $30,000. Her husband in company
with Buffalo Bill, Wild Bill and other delineators of life on the
plains are announced to appear at Williamsport, Pa., on the
8th instant and it may be that Mrs. Omohundro will lend the
aid of her talent to the success of this troupe.

Some time after their marriage the couple purchased the
Suffolk Hall property in Lowell, Mass. This together with
a summer home acquired in nearby Billerica became "home"
to them when not traveling with their shows. When away,
the property was looked after by Miss Angelina Morlacchi,
a sister, who made her home with them in Lowell.

During the first part of the 1874-75 season when her
plainsman husband was hunting with the Earl of Dunraven,
Mlle. Morlacchi and her ballet troupe were again on the
road. The hunt over, Jack returned and resumed his place
as manager of the troupe for the spring and summer tour.

From the middle until the last of June, 1875, at the Boston
Theatre, the troupe presented a Terpisichorean Drama in two
acts, entitled *"La Bayadère,"* interpreted by Mlle. Morlacchi.
The cast included Eugene Clarke, Thomas Bartleman, Adol-
phine Estelle, Russell S. Glover and Cora Andriana. The
dancers were Lizzie Dale, Josie Atkinson, Amelia Huck, May
Bogart, Hattie Smith, Pauline Smith, Saidee Smith, Mlle.
Evers, Emma Mars, Julia Melville, Carrie Prescott, Evaline
Stetson, May Thomas, Addie Hearne, Iola Smiley, Emma
Smiley, Marion Follett, Hattie Follett, Annie Winslow and
Marie Henley.

Ned Crinkle writing in the *New York World* in 1886 pays
a fine tribute to this remarkable woman in these words:

. . . In the height of her beauty and the flush of her power
she had every path of a successful stage queen open to her . . .
I find that the record and the traditions agree as to her exemplary character, her exceptional probity, her marked individ-
uality and her rare sense of honor and justice. Isn't this delicious
in a ballet-dancer? . . . Some of the stories of her independent
character are both refreshing and curious. On one occasion, when
playing in a spectacular piece, she saw the property man care-
lessly break one of the ballet girl's helmets, for which she was

CARD IMPERIAL.

M. H. Omohundro

TEXAS JACK, 1873

A studio photograph of the handsome scout taken shortly after his marriage to Mlle. Morlacchi.

charged $2 and the management deducted it from the girl's salary, in spite of her protests. Indignant M'lle Morlacchi sent for the manager and told him she had seen the property man break the helmet. She insisted that the girl's money should be refunded. When the manager refused, she threw up her engagement, and, leaving the theatre, took the girl with her.

During the Fisk regime at the Grand Opera House, all the efforts to entrap her into the Bohemian orgies utterly failed. To all the polite invitations to supper she invariably sent a polite declination. She saved her money, invested it carefully, and when her husband died she retired on a competence of her own, with a clean record.

One of her early managers, M. B. Leavitt, writing many years later, opined, "I ask, whom have we today to equal or even compare with Fanny Ellsler, Marie Taglioni, Rose Cartio, Rita Sangalli, Josephine Morlacchi . . . in their classic expositions of the high school of dancing" . . .[2]

Indeed Mlle. Morlacchi was a remarkable lady in many ways, and above all a fitting companion and steadying influence upon the adventurous plainsman. If we are to judge from available records, their short life together must have been one of mutual happiness. To Texas Jack she was ever the demure, beautiful and lovable young lady which took his eyes the first night he went on the stage. And to Mlle. Morlacchi Jack was always the gallant and handsome scout to whom she lost her heart that December night in Chicago. What more can be said of true lovers?

[2] M. B. Leavitt in "*Fifty Years of Theatrical Management.*"

8

PLAINSMAN–HUNTER–GUIDE

TEXAS JACK'S life was composed of
many facets, in the most of which he was
more than ordinarily proficient. Outstanding among his
many traits was his extraordinary ability as a plainsman. From
youth he seems to have been gifted with a full measure of
unerring judgment, a qualification of utmost importance to
the successful scout, guide, Indian fighter and hunter.

Had it not been for his innate modesty, the name of Texas
Jack would be much better known today. He was never one
to push himself forward into the spotlight, even in the field
where his ability was pre-eminent. While others gloried in
the limelight he seemed perfectly content to go quietly about
whatever task that needed doing at the time, and to do it
with efficiency and dispatch. Writing in later years, Mrs.
Cody recalls that she saw Texas Jack, "swing off his horse,
tired and dusty from miles in the saddle, worn from days
and nights without sleep, when perhaps the lives of hundreds
depended upon his nerve, his skill with the rifle, his knowledge of the prairies." A close scrutiny of his life and activities
would indicate that he was the best of Buffalo Bill and Wild
Bill rolled into one. He had the cheery, sunny disposition of
Cody plus the cold calculating judgment of Hickok.

A friend and companion of many of the noted plainsmen,
hunters and military men of his day, Texas Jack's ability,
sound judgment and bravery have never been questioned.
Many testify to his exceptional ability as a plainsman. Buffalo
Bill, who was perhaps his closest friend, relied constantly
upon him. The two of them were never happier than when
out on a hunt together. Doc W. F. Carver had been on many

hunts[1] with him and found him to be a splendid shot with
either pistol or rifle, as well as being "a good boy." This
coming from the world's outstanding marksman, as Carver
was for many years, is no small tribute. It was he who referred to Texas Jack as the "Prairie Whirlwind," and called
him one of the best frontiersmen in the West, "full of fun
and the devil, and straight as a die in all things."

The best word pictures of Texas Jack, the plainsman and
guide, have been given by men for whom he served as
guide on hunting expeditions in the West. The Earl of Dunraven, the English hunter of note, gives two interesting
descriptions of Jack. The first taken from his book *Canadian
Nights*[2] tells of his first meeting with the two scouts, Cody
and Omohundro, when he first visited Fort McPherson in
1872. He writes:

In another minute or two they cantered up, swung themselves
out of the saddle, threw their bridles over a post, caught up their
rifles, and stepped onto the platform. I thought I had never seen
two finer-looking specimens of humanity, or two more picturesque figures. Both were tall, well-built, active-looking men, with
singularly handsome features. Bill was dressed in a pair of
corduroys tucked into his high boots, and a blue flannel shirt.
He wore a broad-rimmed felt hat, or sombrero, and a white
handkerchief folded like a little shawl loosely fastened round
his neck, to keep off the fierce rays of the afternoon sun. Jack's
costume was similar, with the exception that he wore moccasins,
and had his lower limbs encased in a pair of greasy deer-skin
trousers, ornamented with fringes along the seams. Round his
waist was a belt supporting a revolver, two butcher knives, and
in his hand he carried his trusty rifle, the "Widow." Jack, tall
and lithe, with light brown close-cropped hair, clear laughing
honest blue eyes, and a soft and winning smile, might have sat
as a model for a typical modern Anglo-Saxon—if ethnologists
will excuse the term * * *

Buffalo Bill and Texas Jack were as fine specimens of their
race and class as could anywhere be found; and that is saying a
great deal, for honest hearts and stalwart frames and handsome
features are not rare among the pioneers of Western civilization.

---

[1] Raymond W. Thorp in *Western Sportsman*, Feb. 1940.
[2] Published by Smith, Elder & Co., London, 1914. Used by special permission of the present copyright owners, John Murray, Ltd., London.

It might be supposed that these hunters, Indian-trackers, cattle-boys, and miners are disagreeable people to come across. That is not the case at all. There are, of course, some rough characters, regular desperados, among them, and they occasionally shoot each other pretty freely in gambling quarrels and drunken sprees; but to a stranger who knows how to behave himself, they are, as far as my experience goes, most civil and obliging. If a man is civil to them they will be civil to him, unless he wants their assistance, and then they will be ready and willing to give it. The manly sense of independence, the self-respect, and the feeling of respect for others engendered by it, which so strongly characterize the American people, are as deeply marked and have as good an effect among the nomads of the West as in any other class of the population * * *

We scoured the country the first couple of days in vain, seeing nothing, not even a fresh sign. On the third afternoon we—that is, myself and a friend and Buffalo Bill—were riding along, somewhat dispirited, a little to the rear of Texas Jack, who had gone on ahead and had disappeared around a hill. Presently we caught sight of him again on a little bluff at some distance from us. He had dismounted, and was running round and round on all fours, making such extraordinary antics that I imagined he had gone suddenly insane, till Buffalo Bill explained that he was merely indicating to us in the language of the plains that there was some wapiti (elk) in sight and pretty near. So we approached him very cautiously, and looking over the edge of the bluff saw a sight which I shall never forget—a herd of at least 120 or 130 wapiti on the little plain below us close to the edge of the river * * *

Next morning a little after sunrise, I was awakened as usual by hearing scratch, scratch, against the canvas of my tent door. "Come in," I said, with a sleepy and somewhat sulky voice at being disturbed, for I could feel by the stiffened and frozen condition of the blankets about my mouth that it was a very cold morning, and I was still tolerably warm. My "come in" was answered by the appearance of Jack's jolly face as he undid the strings that tied the tent door, and came in, rubbing his hands and stamping his feet. "Good morning," says Jack; "It's about time to get up, it's a fine morning, and it's going to be a fine day for hunting." "All right, Jack, I will be up in a minute, in the meantime there is the pannikin, and there is the keg." Jack, like most prairie men, invariably introduced himself to the Sun-god with a copious libation of whiskey. To take a big drink of raw whiskey in the morning, and to touch nothing more during the rest of the day, appears to me a most extraordinary perversion of principle. However, it is a part of the manners and customs of the country, and may be adapted to that peculiar region . . . After Jack had tossed off his tot of whiskey with the customary salutation "How," to which we replied with the polite rejoiner, "drink hearty," we crawled out of our blankets . . .

On August 9, 1874, the following note appeared in the *Rocky Mountain News* (Denver). "Texas Jack," a noted plainsman, is in town. He is to guide the Earl of Dunraven and party on a hunting trip."

Relating the experiences of his second hunt in his book *The Great Divide* [3] the Earl further describes his friend and guide in the following manner:

My first act after making up my mind to undertake the trip to Geyserland was to write to my old friend, hunting companion and guide, Mr. John Omohundro, better known as Texas Jack, and endeavour to secure his services for the expedition. Jack and I in company had run wapiti and buffalo many times upon the plains. I had made his acquaintance some years ago on my first hunt undertaken under the auspices of another celebrated frontier-man, William Cody, well known to Western fame by the sobriquet of Buffalo Bill as an intrepid, trailer of Indians and Government scout. Jack started for me my first bison, a solitary savage old bull, down on one of the tributaries of the Republican; under his auspices I slew my first elk also, and, though it was not a very large one, I thought it the most magnificent animal the world had ever produced. * * *

I had had plenty of experience therefore with Jack, and knew him to be just the man I wanted; but since those merry days among the sandhills and on the plains, he had settled down in life and married; and whether he could be induced to leave his wife and comfortable home and to brave the hardships and dangers of a hunting or exploring trip to the far West, I was very much in doubt. I was therefore much pleased one fine day, as I was lying dozing during the heat of the noon in my tent, pitched close to the never-melting snows on Long's Peak, to receive a letter from Jack, forwarded from the postoffice of the rising little town of Longmont, saying that he was ready for anything, that he would be delighted to come, and was prepared

<del>_____</del>
[3] "*The Great Divide,*" Chatto and Windus, London, 1876.

to accompany me anywhere. He added that I should find him at Charpiot's Restaurant, Denver, in a couple of days. * * *

It was late in the month of July when I got Jack's letter, and, acting upon it, I on the following day bade adieu to the happy hunting-grounds of Estes Park and drove down to Denver, the capital of Colorado, a distance of 60 miles. While still at some distance from the town I became aware of a great coruscation, which I took to proceed from a comet or some other meteorological eccentricity, but which on approaching nearer resolved itself into the diamond shirt-studs and breast-pin shining in the snowy "bosom" of my friend, Texas Jack, who had already arrived from the classic east winds of Boston to share the fortunes of the trip. Pork and beans and pickled cucumbers had failed to sour his genial smile; aesthetic dissipation had not dulled the lustre of his eye. Jack at Denver in broadcloth and white linen was the same Jack that I had last seen upon the North Platte, grimy in an old buckskin suit redolent of slaughtered animals and bodily deliquescence. * * *

Having a great antipathy to stage traveling in promiscuous company, I determined, throwing prudence to the winds, to make myself as comfortable as circumstances would allow, regardless of expense; and accordingly I sent Jack on ahead to Salt Lake City to negotiate terms and charter the entire vehicle for our own sole and particular use, while we took our ease in our inn at Denver. On receiving a telegram from him to say "all right," we joined him at Deseret, and spent a couple of days in that city of saintly sinners, making a few necessary purchases, such as saddles, buffalo robes, and bridles.

Deseret is a very pretty town, beautifully situated on a plain almost surrounded by spurs of the Wahsatch Range. It looks clean from a distance, and on inspection it justifies its appearance . . . I enjoyed myself very well, and was introduced by Jack to many estimable acquaintances, and to many curious scenes. But I am not sure that on the whole I benefited much, pecuniarily, from his assistance.

True, I acquired a considerable amount of second-hand renown, and, like the moon, shown with borrowed splendour, Jack was dressed in beaded buckskins and moccasins, fringed leggings and broad felt hat. Jack is a tall, straight, and handsome man, and in walking through the well-watered streets of Deseret in his company I felt the same proud conscious glow that prevades the white waistcoat of the male debutant when for the first time he walks down St. James Street, arm in arm with the best dressed and most fashionable man about town. It was obvious to all that I was on terms of equality with a great personage, and on that account cigars were frequent and drinks free. But I don't know that there was any great reduction in buffalo robes and saddles. * * *

We bought a pony at Sterling . . . He was a native pony, of mixed Spanish and American blood. Like all half-breed mustangs, he was not destitute of the diabolical accomplishment of "buck-jumping" and he exhibited a slight disposition to indulge in the pastime; but, as he evidently was not a thorough proficient at it, Jack found no difficulty in subduing his early efforts. * * *

Jack, who is of course also smoking—he is always smoking, ex-cept when he is eating, and the few minutes he is obliged to devote to mastication are grudgingly given—is holding forth to the rest of us, telling us some thrilling tale of cattle raids away down by the Rio Grande on the Mexican frontier; graph-ically describing some wild scurry with the Commanches on the plains of Texas; or making us laugh over some utterly absurd story narrated in that comical language and with that quaint dry humour which are peculiar to the American na-tion. * * *

Boteler is lying on his stomach, toasting on a willow-wand a final fragment of meat. He does not use tobacco, and eats all the time that others smoke. He is greatly relishing Jack's story, except when some not over-complimentary allusion to the Yankees comes in; for Boteler served in the Federal Army during the great Civil War, while Jack, Virginian born and raised in Texas, naturally went in for the Southern side. * * *

About one or two in the morning I awake . . . and find the fire burning brightly, and Jack sitting up in bed smoking, for he is of a wakeful disposition, and has been out to look about and put on some fresh fuel . . . We have a smoke and a talk, see what time it is, get sleepy and curl up again. The next time consciousness invades me I hear Jack outside, yawning, stretch-ing, stamping on the ground, and making all manner of strange Indian noises . . . The fire is freshened up. Jack, after the manner of his race, takes a good square honest drink of whisky "straight" while hot coffee dispels the vapour of the night and clears the cobwebs from the brains of the rest of us. * * *

It was a pitch dark night; but Jack, guided by the instincts of an old prairie man, had no difficulty in finding his way, and joined us long before we reached Boteler's, bearing on his saddle a quarter of lamb. * * *

Oh that drive! Can I ever forget it? It occurs to my mind like the memory of some horrid dream—some dreadful nightmare. Four days and four nights in the interior of that vehicle, worse a great deal than Jonah's three in the whale's belly; four mortal days and nights going 340 miles, or thereabouts. We got on pretty well for the first two days, thanks to the unfailing cheerfulness and indomitable good-humor of Jack. * * *

Jack sat beside me on the front seat, his six feet of lissom frame tied and knotted up into inextricable confusion, his head appearing in strange and unexpected places, hands and feet turning up promiscuously, and without the slightest regard to the anatomical position which they are usually supposed to occupy . . . Jack, best and cheeriest of companions, was for once out of humor. Fervent and frequent were his prayers, having reference to the future condition of the driver, horses, coach, road, those that made it, and everybody that had to do with the line.

Dr. George Henry Kingsley, who was one of the members of the Earl of Dunraven's party in 1872 and again in 1874, for which Texas Jack served as guide, later wrote a book, *Notes on Sport and Travel*.[4] His paean of praise of Texas Jack is found in the opening paragraph and contains a bit of interesting information concerning the scout:

Come forth! O Texas Jack, known in the "sorf south" before the war as J. B. Omohundro, Esq.; and would that a better hand than mine were here to paint your portrait! If Buffalo Bill belongs to the school of Charles I, pale, large eyed, and dreamy, Jack, all life, and blood, and fire, blazing with suppressed poetry, is Elizabethan to the back bone! He too is an eminently handsome man, and the sight of him in his fringed hunting buckskins, short hunting shirt decorated with patches of red and blue stained leather, pair of delicate white moccasins embroidered by the hand of some aesthetic and loving squaw, with his short, bright brown curls covered by a velvet cap with a broad gold band around it, would play the very mischief with many an eastern girl's heart * * *

Jack raves poetically as we canter along side by side, and on one of us remarking what a deal of beauty there is in the most plain prairie, he bursts out, "Ah! you should see it in the springtime, with the antelopes feeding in one direction, the buffaloes in another, and the little birdies boo-hooing around, building their nesties, and raising hell generally!"

---

[4] Published by Macmillian and Company, London. Used by special permission.

Jack, being a southern man, thinks it necessary to suppose that he has Indian blood in his veins, a very popular idea in those parts. If he has, he is rather rough on his relatives, for he is deadly on Indians. Indian hunting is, in fact, the real profession of both Jack and Bill, they being retained as trackers, aye, and as fighters too, in the case of horses being run from the neighbourhood of the Fort; though, from time to time, they are put in charge of a band to see that it does not exceed the limits of its Reservation, and to lead it out to the hunt as a shepherd leadeth his flock to the pasture. They have the strangest feelings about Indians, these two. Though, when on the war path, they would no more hesitate to shoot down an Indian off his Reservation, than they would hesitate to throw a stone at a felonious chipmunk, they have a sympathy and a tenderness towards them infinitely greater than you will find among the greedy, pushing settlers, who regard them as mere vermin who must be destroyed for the sake of the ground on which depends their very existence. But these men know the Indian and his almost incredible wrongs, and the causes which have turned him into the ruthless savage that he is, and often have I heard of their class say that, before God, the Indian was in the right, and was only doing what any American citizen would do in his place. It is not so much that the intentions of the U. S. Government are not good, as it is that the manner in which they are carried out is extremely evil. The men who are told off as Indian agents are notorious for their wholesale peculations, and for the riches which they amass; and the wretched native, driven to desperation, and knowing that death is certain, chooses to meet it his own way, and makes it as sweet as he can with revenge.

Hunting, too, offers its amusing aspects as this brief incident related to Gen. D. H. Maury will disclose. He writes of one night in Montgomery, Alabama, when General John G. Walker, Texas Jack and himself were seated together talking of their experiences on the plains, and how they found they had all had the same experience with their first buffalo. Jack related that after shooting his first one, he rushed up to stick his knife into it. Just then the animal sprang up and took out after him. Making tracks Jack put a wagon between him and the enraged beast only to find the buffalo had dropped dead just as it lowered its head to charge the wagon.[5]

---

[5] "*Recollections of a Virginian*," published by Charles Scribner's Sons, New York, 1894.

SPIRIT OF THE TIMES

OF THE

"THE SPIRIT OF THE TIMES"

"SHALL TEACH ME SPEED"
King John Act IV.

TWENTY-FOUR PAGES

A Chronicle of the Turf, Field Sports, Aquatics, Agriculture, and the Stage

VOL. 93—No. 1
NUMBER 3 PARK ROW.

NEW YORK, SATURDAY, FEBRUARY 10, 1877.

SUBSCRIPTION:
FIVE DOLLARS A YEAR

SCENE FROM "FIFTH AVENUE," AT BOOTH'S THEATRE.

"SPIRIT OF THE TIMES," 1877

"The American Gentleman's Newspaper" of the seventies, for which
Texas Jack wrote a few articles on his experiences. He was in turn
interviewed by their reporters and given a full page feature story.

Col. Charles D. Randolph "Buckskin Bill"
TEXAS JACK, Scout, 1872
The youthful scout as he appeared while living at Cottonwood Springs.

For a definite description of hunting in the frontier days, we are indebted to Texas Jack himself. Writing in 1877 for the magazine, *Spirit of the Times,* he vividly describes some of his hunting experiences on the plains and in Florida. Two of the articles "A Chapter from Texas Jack" and "A Chat with Texas Jack" are in the nature of interviews while two others, "Hunting Deer in Florida" and "My First Buffalo Hunt with Indians," are the product of his own pen. Taken from their original source, they are included here for the illumination they throw on the renowned scout and early day hunting:

A CHAPTER FROM TEXAS JACK[6]

"Well, what do you want to see me about?" said Texas Jack, the great hunter and Indian-fighter, as he walked into our offices

---

[6] *Spirit of the Times,* Feb. 10, 1877.

the other day, a picture of a Western scout, with his tall sinewy form, bronzed face, flowing locks, and head covered with a broad-brimmed sombrero. Taking a seat on our invitation, and a light for his cigar on his own, he repeated the request.

"Why," said we, "you have been having a long hunt with those English fellows; you know lots of things that other people don't and we would like to have you unload yourself for the benefit of the readers of *The Spirit.* If you will only get to talking, we'll take care of printing it."

"Well, there isn't much to say about that hunt. You see, Sir John Reid and his cousin, Mr. Eaton, were about the most sensible men and best hunters I ever piloted over the plains. They were

HUNTING FOR TROPHIES

more than anything else, and didn't kill any game and leave it to rot on the ground. Probably you would like to have me tell you just how we occupied ourselves during a day, for the days were pretty much alike, though we were out about three months, in the Sweetwater Country, Wyoming Territory. There were seven of us in the party: two Englishmen, myself, my assistant hunter, Tom Sun, better known as "Indian Tom," a Frenchman, and a

GREAT INDIAN FIGHTER;

a servant for the Englishmen, a wagon-driver, and a cook. We didn't take much provisions with us, as we killed all our fresh meat. In the morning, I always made it my first business to hustle out Sir John and his cousin. They always seemed in a hurry, but they were always late in getting to the hunt, and liked their blankets in the morning. After breakfast we would get on the ponies—little Indian ponies called bronchos, and I tell you they are rascals. I always rode one called Snort, that could kick the hat off your head while you were on his back. Here's a letter I just got from Tom Sun, telling about Robert, the English servant, trying to ride him since I left the plains. Snort threw him three times in as many minutes, and Roberts said he was

"A BLOODY BEAST."

Robert rode in the English style, but found it wouldn't work with mustangs. Well, the game we were after was elk, black-tail deer, antelope, and mountain sheep. The bear were all holed up for the winter, as we started out late in the season. The elk we'd find on the flats, away from the mountains, browsing.

Sometimes there would be two or three thousand head in a band, most of them being does and fawns, with a few bucks scattered around. In a band of three thousand head there would be not more than thirty or forty bucks, for these elk have

MORE WIVES THAN BRIGHAM YOUNG.

When we would sight a band a long way off, the first thing would be to dispute whether they were Indians or elk, for the critters, with their antlers, look at a distance like men on horseback. We didn't see any Indians, though, all the time we were out, and I wasn't a bit sorry for that. After we got near enough to see plainly, we would look for such antlers as we wanted, and would go for those. The best antlers are on the old, lone bucks, who get driven away from the bands, generally; sometimes we would find them in the bands. Elk are about the

STUPIDEST ANIMALS IN THE WORLD,

and you can get all you want by either sneak-hunting or stalking. When they first see you, they are so silly they will walk right toward you, but at a shot they start off, always in the face of the wind, so that they can smell ahead and see behind. Their

NATURAL GAIT IS A TROT;

when they are hurried and frightened, they sometimes break into a clumsy run, but they can't travel near as fast that way. I have timed elk trotting eight miles in twenty-four minutes, over rough ground. When you get a band started, you charge into them, ride your ponies into the midst of the animals, press those you don't want aside by pushing their flanks with your hand, and make for those with fine antlers. They never show fight to men, but are the timidest beasts in the world. The only danger you are in, is that your horse might stumble, and then you would be

TRAMPLED TO DEATH BY THEIR SHARP HOOFS.

Often you can ride around a band of them, and as they will stop for the young ones and wounded ones to join the herd, you can get ahead of them, and take another shot. This was the way our party hunted, for we were after big horns, and not a lot of meat. By sneak-hunting, one man can kill a whole band of elk. He must first get a good stand, in easy range, to leeward of the game, so that he is completely hid, and must kill one with his first shot. They stand then for short time, with their backs humped up and hair raised, looking around to

see in which direction to run. Finally, the leader will make a
break in one direction or another. Now is the important moment.
If the hunter makes a good shot, and kills this leader, the whole
band are at his mercy. Having made one break, and found danger
in that direction, their wits are exhausted, and they just stand
huddled together, and one man, if he has ammunition enough,
could

KILL A THOUSAND OF THEM.

Black-tail deer are just the same, but white-tail deer will run
from the sound of the gun. This style of hunting is called getting
a stand on the game. You can get a stand on buffalo, and they
will act the same as the elk, I have killed thirty-five buffalo out
of a herd in this way, and only stopped because I was tired."

"Hasn't there been some complaint of parties of hunters from
abroad slaughtering game needlessly?"

"Oh, yes; but I don't think there has been much of that
sort of thing done lately. I know our party killed nothing but
what they wanted, and these Englishmen were good shots, and
brought down a buck when they drew a bead on him. There
is a fine of $50 for leaving any game on the ground. Capt.
Shaw, an Englishman who was hunting to the north of us,
did kill forty or fifty old buck elk, which he left, but that was
really a service to the country. Their meat was no good, and
they only worry the young bucks. You see, these elk are mighty
queer beasts. A buck is

NO ACCOUNT IN THE HERD

after he is three year old for getting fawns, and the young
bucks have antlers with a single prong, while these big antlers,
such as you saw at Overton's, belong to the old played-out
fellows. These antlers are full grown about September every
year, and are shed every February, and an old buck has to devote
about three-quarters of the year to getting rid of his old set, and
putting on his new. They have pretty bad times over it. The
elk seeks a lonely place, where he can lie down and reach
water by sticking his nose out, and can get grass without
scarcely moving. Likely he

WON'T STIR A QUARTER OF A MILE

during an entire winter. When the new antlers begin to come,
they are very tender at first, with blood at the points, and
covered with a kind of skin. If he happens to touch them
against anything, it hurts like pulling a tooth. So he passes
week after week, with his nose in a stream and his rump against

a rock, doing nothing but nurse his horns, until it gets to be August, when they have nearly got their growth. Then some fine day he takes a scrape on something, and off comes the covering from his antlers, and then he sharpens the points on the trees or rocks, and

BEGINS TO FEEL HIS OATS.

He gives himself a big shake, and starts on the rampage, trumpeting as he goes. About this time of the year the plains are full of these cries. I tell you, it's a good thing to kill these old pestilences, for they are no use to themselves or anybody else. It isn't hunters that are making game scarce out West, by any means. It's the ignorant emigrants, who

SCARE THE GAME, AND DON'T KILL IT.

These people keep popping away, without hitting anything, and frighten the animals so that they go into country that is strange to them, where they don't know how to find grass and water, and they starve; and that is why so many skeletons bleach the prairies of the West. Your hunter, if he doesn't want a deer, leaves him, and can kill one without disturbing those grazing in the next cañon; but bunglers manage, without slaughtering much, to drive the game into an unfit country. You see, the elk and the deer and the buffalo can't stand civilization, and are perishing fast; but the antelopes seem to like a little human society, and are increasing in numbers."

"You say that elk are so timid; is that the case with most of the game in the West?"

"Yes, all but the bear. He is the most contrary chap in the world. Elk, buffalo, deer, wolves, you do anything to frighten them, fire a gun, or come upon them suddenly, and they will run away, but a bear

WILL GO FOR YOU.

Old hunters don't want to have any truck with bears. They are always spoiling for a fight, and are so strong and cunning, and swift, and hard to kill, that a man is pretty sure to get the worst of it if he tackles one of them. It was just true what California Joe said, that "The best place to hunt bears was where there wasn't any." A grizzly will stand in the middle of the road, growling and getting his mad up, when there isn't a live creature within forty miles of him. If you meet one and turn out for him, he will probably leave you alone; but if you say a word, look out for him. Many a time I have just made some such remark to a bear as "Where are you going, Tommy?"

when, in an instant his arms would be up, and be ready to tear me to pieces. No, sir, we don't go bear-hunting very much, and are willing to cry quits with those fellows. You see they can run as fast as a horse, and you have to put a bullet into just such a place to kill them, and until they are dead they are dangerous. Tom Sun got treed on a rock by a grizzly once, and the old loafer just waited there at the foot of the rock for twenty-four hours before he made up his mind to walk off. Tom didn't dare shoot, because his rifle was a light one, and he was afraid he might fail to kill the bear, who would then have quietly wiped him off the rock and clawed him to bits. They are the most impudent beggers, and presume on their privileges. Often a big grizzly will walk into camp, as uncon- cerned as you please, stroll up to a tree where the game is hanging, help himself to what he wants, and go away. Nobody interferes with him. If he is satisfied to go off with the meat, the hunters are satisfied to let him. I have seen a bear walking along, with an entire elk carcass, with the antlers on, weighing as much as eight hundred pounds, tucked under his arm.

A BEAR IN A RANCHE

Sometimes one of these fellows visits a ranche when the party is out hunting, and then, I tell you, he makes a mess. They are as mischievous as monkeys, and have no end of curi- osity. Likely the first thing he tackles is a cask of syrup. He gets a little of the dripping from the spigot on his paw, tastes it, says, 'That's good,' whacks in the head of the cask, and pulls it over his head and shoulders, sticking himself all up, but most of the syrup gets into his stomach. Then he finds some tobacco, tastes it, says, "No good," and scatters it over the floor. Next comes a sack of flour. He busts through the cloth with his paw, tastes it, says, "Pretty good," but he don't like it much, so he spreads that all around amongst the tobacco, and he adds to the mess blankets, clothes, everything there is in the hut. Bye-and-bye his stomach gets uneasy from too much molasses, and he lies down and takes a roll, and gets himself all plastered over with flour and tobacco. About the time the hunters come home, perhaps, he has got ready to go, and they meet him in the road, the most comical looking beast you can imagine. He knows he looks queer, but he walks along as much as to say, "No matter what I look like, I'm a bear, and you had better leave me alone; I've got my belly full of sorghum, and don't want any meat, but clear the road for me, or there'll be trouble." When you get inside, you find there is no comfort there, and likely have to travel fifty miles to get something to eat. He has ransacked everything, and spoiled everything.

LASSOING A CINNAMON

I was once out with a party in Texas, and we came across a big cinnamon bear. We all proposed to leave him alone, but there was one fellow who didn't know as much bear as the rest, and he proposed to capture him with his lasso. We told him of the hazards, but he was determined, and, sure enough, he made a good throw, and got the loop around the bear's neck. When old Cinnamon felt it get tight, what do you think he did? He just sat up on his haunches, felt of the rope with one paw, and then began pulling it in, hand over hand. There was a horse and a man fast to the other end of the rope, but

THEY HAD TO COME,

both of them. As for the hunter, he jumped off, and got away, but the bear drew the pony right up to him, and let his bowels out with one blow of his paw. We killed him afterwards, but that chap never tried lassoing any more cinnamons. No, they're poor hunting, are bears. There are about twenty varieties of them, and the hog-backed grizzly is the worst, but they're all cross."

TEXAS JACK ON THE INDIAN QUESTION

"How is it about the Indians?"

"Well, they all seem to have gone North, and I reckon are up to the Canada line. We didn't see any Indian signs all the time we were out. You see the buffalo have all been driven North, and the Indians have to follow them, for they can't be on the war-path without buffalo. They don't like elk, and deer, and small game well enough to live on it, but give them plenty of buffalo meat and they are happy. You know they consider them as their own property. A redskin will speak of buffalo as "my cattle," and as long as they can swell around, on horseback, in paint and feathers, and kill one of their cattle whenever they want food, they're mean; but cut them off from this, and they'll soon come into the agencies, get beef and beans, and be good Indians. The wild Indian and the buffalo are pards, and when one dies the other must. If the Government had put all its soldiers to killing buffalo, instead of trying to kill redskins, and getting butchered themselves, the Indian question would have been settled long ago. But (looking at the clock), bless my soul, how long I've been yarning! Guess I've unloaded myself, sure enough."

9

FRONTIER REPORTER

It IS gratifying that Texas Jack's unusual talents included an ability to adequately describe his own experiences as well as life on the frontier. It is because of this fact that his writings are being used in their entirety.

The graphic account related here concerns the time Texas Jack was shipwrecked in the Gulf of Mexico and ended upon the coast of Florida, and his subsequent hunting experience.

HUNTING DEER IN FLORIDA [1]

Philadelphia, Feb. 23, 1877

DEAR SPIRIT:

As I promised to tell you something about deer hunting in Florida, here goes. I don't know if it will be particularly interesting to you, but it was to me at the time, the peculiar manner of hunting with trained dogs. This section of the country is a desolate pine-forest, low rolling sand-hills, covered with tall trees, beneath which grows a kind of light prairie-grass. The ravines are from fifty to two hundred yards wide, so thick with under-brush, that you couldn't stick a butcher's knife into them, and so swampy that they would bog a saddle-blanket, and are generally bordered by an open savannah that gives a beautiful shot at the startled game as they break for the hills. Occasionally there is an island formation of cane "tussocks," or dry spots, around ancient stumps of trees. These the deer seek to lie on in the daytime, and if it were not for the "bell dog," a regiment of Pinkerton's detectives would never "tumble to," or spot his graceful lordship. When the deer are not in the brush, where they feel safe, they are hard to approach, as the pine-forest are like thinned-out parks, and a clear view can be had, sometimes for a mile or more; a horse therefore, won't do for the woods, and much less for the edges of the boggy swamps. So from camp "shank's pony," the "bell," and slow "track dogs" are our reliances.

---

[1] *Spirit of the Times*, March 3, 1877.

When the swamp is reached where we intend to drive, the "bell-dog," with his little bell around his neck, is started down the centre, and we separate, one hunter or party on each side; the "bell" is thoroughly trained to go slowly, and by the tinkling the hunters can keep opposite him, and each other; and if delayed by any obstruction a signal (a peculiar cluck) he will stop until ordered on. "Slow Track" is trained quietly to follow at the hunter's heels until a shot is fired, which is his signal for business.

Slowly we creep along, guns cocked, eyes strained forward, watching for a startled break (some old bucks are mighty cunning, though I have seen them sneak out a quarter of a mile ahead), when by the hasty rattling of "Bell's" warning we know he has scented, then a startling yelp, a racket in the bush and "look out here they come;" "Which side?" works up the "fever," when, like a streak of greased lightning, deer and dog come tearing into view, and then—"Well,, that depends," as Indian Tom says. If the deer stops suddenly and reposes, all right; if not "Bell's" tinkler is stopped with leaves, and he is sent to the rear, and "Slow Track" is ordered to the front. With great delight he goes scenting for blood, and, if none is found, hide yourself in shame, for all the disgust imaginable will be pictured on that dog's "phsog;" but, if successful, and you have made a "hit," a low whine of laughing pleasantness tells the tale.

Just in advance of us goes "Slow Track," following the bloody trail as cautiously as if stepping on eggs, and happy in visions of a feast on paunch, blood and entrails. Thus we proceed, until the wounded animal is found, "Slow Tracks" being careful not to raise him out of gunshot.

When dispatched, his heart and liver (with some sweet potatoes we always carry) form an immediate lunch, which is invariably enlivened by the jealous wrangling of "Bell" and "Slow Track," whose rivalry is bitter and eternal. A Florida Returning Board could never settle their disputed rights.

The deer is hung up in a tree, where he can be reached with a pack horse, and the hunt proceeds. If you have no packhorse, do as I have done, "tote" him on your back to camp, five or ten miles. It is hard on the back, but good on the appetite. A wounded deer is seldom lost with a "Slow Track," and a humane hunter will always secure the wounded, if possible. I have lost many a fine day's hunting since, on the Plains, in trying to find a wounded animal.

The deer are the white-tail species, and are seldom more than four or five in a band, and twenty-eight is the most I have started in a day's drive. The dogs mostly trained are the ordinary deerhound, or a cross breed of the same with spaniel or some kind of water dog.

Hunting in other sections of the State varies from this mode. Further south, and along the small islands, no dogs are used. We lie in wait near the "licks," or "water holes," and I have set perched in a small palmetto scrub-tree that grows there, for hours and hours, and got no deer. There is but little science and less fun in that, so I did not follow it long.

Fire hunting is a midnight sport, where the boys stay "out all night till broad daylight, and go home with (out sometimes) deer in the morning." I have known several of the "natives" that lost valuable milch cows, and it is well to pursue your hunting far from the settlements, owing to the prejudices thus produced. Owing to the peculiarly wild construction of the country, I believe deer will exist for many years to come.

Well, this is getting too long to particularize other game, but there are bears, catamounts, panthers, wild hogs, turkey, and all variety of water fowls, alligators by the thousand, and the stupidest of all living creatures, though excellent eating, much prized, and generally weighing from twelve to eighteen pounds, named the "gopher," but why I could never tell, for I never saw one "go for" anything. He is hard to describe, a sort of a turtle, lives on the high, dry sand hills, seems never to explore ten feet from his hole, and whose general mode of life is a conundrum. They are caught by "pitting," a pit being dug near their holes, into which they tumble, and are incapable of making any exertion to get out. A pitter was once asked, "What are you digging for?" He answered, "Gopher." "Will you get him?" "Get him, of course I'll get him; I am out of meat." The men who hunt for them are considered as lazy as they. As the same feeling is gradually coming over me, and may be affecting you, I will close, with "so long," for the present.

The following story, like the one entitled, "The Cow Boy," in a previous chapter, was picked up in the years following the death of Texas Jack, and adapted to fit the whims of whoever was using it at the time. Credit was usually given, but the names were changed for one reason or another. Taken from the original source, it is reprinted here just as Texas Jack wrote it; for it, too, has become a classic of plains lore.

MY FIRST BUFFALO HUNT WITH INDIANS [2]

Philadelphia, March 5, 1877

DEAR SPIRIT:

The other evening my old friend, Donald McKay, famed at the time of the Modoc War as chief of scouts for Gen. Crook, paid me a visit; and as "speaking of shad reminds me of fish," the occasion brought to my memory my first "buffalo hunt with Indians. If I don't get like the butcher's calf, and "kind o' give out." I'll try and give you an idea of one of the most exciting scenes I ever saw or read of, not excepting my school-boy impression of Andy Jackson's hoo-doo at New Orleans. I thought I had seen fun in a Texas cattle stampede, been astonished in a mustang chase; but it wasn't a marker, and it made me believe that Methuselah was right when he suggested that the oldest could "live and learn." It is a pity the old man didn't stick it out. He could have enjoyed this lesson.

A few years ago I was deputized United States Agent, under Major Troth, to accompany a hunting party of Pawnee and Ponca Indians. Although "blanket Indians" (living wild), they have for a long time been great friends of the Government, and have done excellent service under the command of the justly celebrated Major Frank North, whose famed Pawnee scouts have always been a terror to the Sioux nation. Owing to their hatred of each other it is necessary to send an agent with them to prevent "pinics" and also to settle disputes with the white hunters. As Major North was in poor health at that time, this delicate task fell to me.

As I don't like to be long-winded, I'll pass over the scenes and incidents of wild Indian camp-life, the magnificent sight of a moving village of three thousand of "nature's children," looking like a long rainbow in the bright colors of their blankets, beads, feathers, war paint, etc., as it would keep us up all night. It required eleven days to make the march from the Loup River Reservation to Plum Creek, on the North Platte, where our runners reported.

Early in the evening as we were about making camp, my old friend, Baptiste, the interpreter, joyfully remarked, "Jack, the blanket is up three times—fun and fresh meat tomorrow."

There was a great pow-wow that night, and all the warriors were to turn out for the grand buffalo surround, leaving the squaws and papooses in the village. Just before daybreak, there

---

[2] *Spirit of the Times*, March 17, 1877.

was a general stir and bustle on all sides, giving evidence of
the complete preparations making for the coming event. As it
was dark, I busied myself in arranging my own outfit, thinking
of the grand sight soon to be witnessed, and wondering how I
(will) "pan out" in the eyes of my "red brothers." I had not
noticed the manner of their own arrangements in an important
particular that I will hereafter allude to.

At a given signal all started, and when the first blue streaks
of dawn allowed the moving column to be visible, I had time to
make an inspection of the strange cavalcade, and note peculiarities.
I saw at once the "white brother" was at a disadvantage.

I had started fully equipped—bridle, saddle, lariat, rifle, pistol,
belt, etc.—and astride my pony. They, with as near nothing in
garments as Adam and Eve, only breech clout and moccasins, no
saddle, no blanket, not even a bridle, only a small rope, light
bow and a few arrows in hand—in fact not an ounce of weight
more than necessary, and unlike myself, all scudding along at a
marvellous rate, leading their fiery ponies, so as to reserve every
energy for the grand event in prospect.

Taking it all in at a glance, your "humble servant," quite
abashed, let go all holts and slipped off his critter, feeling that
the Bronco looked more like a government pack mule. I at
once mentally gave up the intention of paralyzing my light
rigged side pards in the coming contest. As they were all walking,
I thought the buffalo were quite near; but what was my astonishment, as mile after mile was scored, that I gradually found
myself dropping slowly but surely behind, and, so as not to
get left, compelled every now and then to mount and lope to
the front, there to perceive from the twinkling eyes of friend
"Lo" a smile that his otherwise stolid face gave no evidence of.
How deep an Indian can think, and it not be surface plain,
I believe has never been measured. Just imagine this "lick" kept
up with apparent ease by them for fully eighteen or twenty
miles, and you may get a partial idea of your friend Jack's
tribulations.

Fortunately, I kept up, but at what an expense of muscle,
verging on a complete "funk," you can only appreciate by
indulging in a similar spin.

About this time a halt occurred, and you can bet I was mighty
glad of it. Suddenly two of three scouts dashed up. A hurried
council was held, during which the pipe was passed. Everything
now seemed arranged, and, after a little further advance, again
a halt, when amid great but suppressed excitement, every Indian

mounted his now almost frantic steed, each eagerly seeking to edge his way without observation to the front.

About two hundred horses, close abreast in the front line; say one hundred and fifty wedging in half way between, formed a half second line; and one hundred struggling for place, a third line; the chiefs in front gesticulating, pantomiming, and with slashing whips, keeping back the excited mass, whose plunging, panting ponies, as impatient as their masters, fretted, frothed, and foamed—both seemed moulded into one being, with only one thought, one feeling, one ambition, as with flashing eye they waited for the signal, "Go," to let their pent-up souls speed on to the honors of the chase.

Their prey in fancied security, now quietly browsing to the windward in a low, open flat, some half mile wide and two or three miles long, on top of a high divide, concealed from view by risings and breaks. Gradually they approach the knoll, their heads reach its level, the backs of the buffalo are seen, then a full view, when Pi-ta-ne-sha-a-du (Old Peter, the head chief) gives the word, drops the blanket, and they are "off."

Whew! Wheeze! Thunder and lightning! Jerome Parks, and Hippodromes! Talk of tornadoes, whirlwinds, avalanches, water-spouts, prairie fires, Niagara, Mount Vesuvius (and I have seen them all except old Vesuve); boil them all together, mix them well, and serve on one plate, and you will have a limited idea of the charge of this "light brigade." They fairly left a hole in the air. With a roar like Niagara, the speed of a whirlwind, like the sweep of a tornado, the rush of a snowslide, the suddenness of a water-spout, the rumbling of Vesuvius, with the fire of death in their souls, they pounce on their prey, and in an instant, amid a cloud of dust, nothing is visible but a mingled mass of flying arrows, horses' heels, buffaloes' tails, Indian heads, half of ponies, half of men, half of buffalo, until one thinks it a dream, or a heavy case of the "jim-jams."

I just anchored in astonishment. Where are they? Ah, there is one; then another, a third, a fourth. Over the plains in all directions they go, as the choice meat hunters cut them out, while in a jumbled mass, circling round and round in the main body. The clouds of dust gradually rise as if a curtain lifted, horses stop as buffalo drop, until there is a clear panoramic view of a busy scene, all quiet, everything still (save a few fleet ones in the distance); horses riderless, browsing proudly, conscious of success; the prairie dotted here, there, everywhere in all directions with dead bison; and happy, hungry, hunters skinning, slashing, cutting the late proud monarch of the plains.

I was so interested in the sight that I came near being left, when fortunately a lucky long-range shot (the only one fired during the day) at a stray heifer saved my reputation. In about two hours every pony was loaded, their packing being quite a study that would need a deserved and lengthy description. It was wonderful.

As I had "a heap of walk out," I proposed to ride in, so I took a small cut of choice meat—a straight cut—for camp. Every pony was packed down only mine, seeing which "Peter's Pap-poose" (the Sun Chief) invited himself up behind me. Talk of gall, an Indian has got more cheek than a government mule! He laughed at my objections, but as he had loaned me the pony I had to submit. He even directed the gait, and kept up a continual jabbering of "Wisgoots, ugh! de-goinartsonse starkees, ugh!" which I afterwards learned meant "Hurry up, I am tired, hungry, and dry—how!"

The summer of 1876 was permeated with news of Indian uprisings and battles. Signal fires were burning and the Sioux were again on the warpath. In June Custer and his entire command were wiped out at the battle of the Little Big Horn. Other Cavalry and Army Units were on the march. It was to cover such frontier activities as these that *The New York Herald* sent Texas Jack out as a scout and reporter. One of Jack's friends, Capt. Jack, (the poet scout) also did some work for the same paper during this time. His work involved the carrying of dispatches from the field to the nearest telegraph office, and he is noted for one particular ride on which he "scooped" other papers in getting his dispatches on the wire first. Since Texas Jack was a reporter-scout for the paper, it is believed that many of the dispatches Capt. Jack carried were those written by Jack himself.

In his Autobiography, Buffalo Bill tells of meeting his old friend in this capacity. He says, "So I started down the river on the steamer *Yellowstone* enroute to Fort Buford. On the same morning Generals Terry and Crook pulled out for Powder River, to take up the old Indian trail which we had recently left. The steamer had proceeded down the stream about twenty miles when it was met by another boat on its way up the river, having on board General Whistler and some fresh troops for General Terry's command. Both boats landed, and almost the first person I met was my old friend and partner, Texas Jack, who had been sent out as a dispatch carrier for *The New York Herald*."

A few weeks after this, a young lieutenant by the name of Hugh L. Scott was on his way to the troubled frontier to join up with the Seventh Cavalry. In St. Paul at the Merchants Hotel he met two officers of the Seventh Cavalry, Captains Benteen and MacDougal who had recently returned from the Yellowstone. At the time Benteen was quite a hero. It was he who was credited with saving some remnants of the Seventh Cavalry. With these two officers was a picturesque man with long dark hair and dressed in bucksin. He was introduced to the young Lieutenant as "Texas Jack" Omohundro. It was an incident that made a lasting impression on Lieut. Scott because it was his first introduction to one of the frontier scouts.[3]

Texas Jack's reporting for the New York newspaper has been mentioned in other writings, but this is believed to be the first time this feature article under his own name has ever been reprinted since it first appeared in the September 30, 1876, issue of *The New York Herald*.

TEXAS JACK ON THE INDIAN WAR

The following interesting story is told by Mr. John Omohundro, more familiarly known as Texas Jack, the famous scout who has just arrived from the frontier:

I left on the morning of the 4th of August, and after stopping at Philadelphia to take a hasty farewell of my wife, proceeded via Chicago and St. Paul to Bismark, where I purchased an outfit, a pony and a pack mule. At that time there was no certainty as to where the army was. It had left *The Rosebud* and no news had been received of its movements. I determined to go up the Yellowstone as far as I could by boat and then take to the country with my pony and pack mule. I took the steamer *Josephine* on the evening of the 15th of August, and we started on our journey in company with another boat, *the*

---

[3] Maj. Gen. Hugh L. Scott, in "*Some Memories of a Soldier*," The Century Company, New York, 1928.

Yellowstone. General Whistler was on our boat with two companies of infantry, and another on *The Yellowstone.* His errand was the same as my own, to learn the whereabouts of the army, and if possible, join it. We moved up the river as far as Fort Buford, where we arrived on the 18th. There we learned that the Indians had fired into the boat which went ahead of us a few miles below Buford, on the Missouri River. There was great excitement among the people there. They had run off some woodchopper's stock and created great alarm. Nothing could be learned of the whereabouts of the army here. The first news we got was on the 20th, when we met some half dozen soldiers in a small boat, from whom we learned that Terry's entire command was at or near the mouth of the Powder River, within twenty miles of us. This was good news, but things changed when we learned that both sides of the river were lined with Indians. They had not, however, fired into the soldiers. We continued on our journey without disturbance, and tied up that night without any preparation for defense except a temporary guard to protect the pilot. It was a fortunate thought, for a bullet afterward struck the pilot house and would have killed him but for the protection it afforded. The next morning I got on shore to follow some deer that had run to an island, and found some fresh Indian trails. Coming out of the timber I went to the open sand bar, and got there just in time to see a volley fired into *the Yellowstone* from the opposite side of the river. She was about a quarter of a mile from our boat, and coming toward us. I was directly in range of the firing from the other shore, and could see the bullets skipping along the water. She was not more than eighty or a hundred yards from the shore, and I could see the smoke curling up from the high bluff banks of the river. Other Indians were discovered a little further below and near *the Josephine.* I ran to the brush and made my way hurriedly back to her. There was so much noise and bustle on board that they had not heard the firing. On my way I saw Indians on our side of the river and had to hasten for fear of being cut off. Just as I got aboard, *the Yellowstone* came up alongside of us and reported what had happened. There was one man lying dead on her deck, and several bullets had passed through her. The Indians soon made their appearance again on the bluff immediately opposite, not more than 300 yards off, and we sent a volley into them from both boats that drove them off. No more of them were seen on our side, and hasty breastworks were thrown up around the boats.

We had no means of estimating their numbers. Two or more at a time might be seen riding, and a head or two would look out over a bank, but that was all. Some of the soldiers reported that they saw one or two fall and others lift and carry them off. Later reports showed that a large village had been encamped behind the bluff. We remained behind for three or four hours, till all of them had disappeared, and then steamed up the river a short distance and camped for the night. The next morning, six or eight miles further up the river, we picked up a wounded man and a small boat lying on the shore. The man was bleeding and exhausted. He was barely able to tell his story, and proved to be a deserter from Terry's command. He and a companion deserted together, and the evening before became separated in a chase by some Indians. During the night he returned to find his friend; his body was scalped and cut into pieces.

On the 23rd we met the steamer *Carol* coming down from Terry's old camp near the mouth of the Powder River. She reported that Crook had left the day before and Terry that day, moving in a southerly direction. Dispatches were at once sent from our boat to Terry. He reported back, ordering all further movements of boats and wagons stopped. His command came up the next day, the 24th, and crossed over to us. Crook in the meantime was to follow the main trail, leading about east, and then bearing off south toward the Little Missouri. After remaining two days in camp, Terry's command marched off nearly northwest from the Yellowstone River, and, after making a big detour, arrived again at Glen Dive, on the river, about half way between Buford and the mouth of the Powder River, expecting to meet Crook there or encounter the Indians, he might drive to cross the Yellowstone. Colonel Rice, who was entrenched at Glen Dive, reported that no Indians had been seen for several days and nothing had been heard of Crook, who we confidently expected to meet. We remained several days in camp, but could learn nothing of him. Colonel Reno took command and commenced a march down the Yellowstone, with the general understanding that we were going to Buford. Terry and his staff, after remaining with us during the first day's march, went on by boat. When within thirty-five miles of Buford a courier reached us with dispatches that the hostile Indians were crossing the Missouri at Wolf's Point, about 150 miles northwest of us. We turned and marched after them. When within fifty miles or so of the place we turned to the river and went the rest of the way by it, arriving at Wolf Point, about eighteen miles below Fort Peck, after a hard march. Two miles below

Wolf Point we found fresh trails and bull boats, which the Indians had used for crossing the river. The boats had been taken back to the side from which they had crossed and left there, as if others were expected to follow. About half a mile further below, before we came to the boats and trails, two Indians appeared on shore and made signs of peace. They said they saw the large moving column and came to see what it was, fearing we were hostiles and in that case not wishing to let us cross. They were, no doubt, runners for the hostiles to spy out our movements, because runners left Buford the moment our movements became known there. They were unsuccessfully pursued by a lieutenant and two scouts, and the two we met were very likely from Buford.

From the traders and friendly Indians at Wolf's Point we found that Long Dog's band of twenty-three lodges had crossed the river several days before and were making for Cypress Mountain, near the Canadian line. They acknowledged at Wolf's Point that at one time we were so close to them that they were compelled to fly with bare ponies and guns, leaving everything else behind them. When I found this out it confirmed a belief I had at one time that we were near them. While making the detour to Glen Dive we came on a herd of moving buffaloes and began a promiscuous firing on them. An old Montana scout named White and myself went off some distance to have a shot by ourselves. Pretty soon I took down a cow and calf at about 150 yards' range and was about to go on and secure some of the meat when I became suspicious, for what reason I could hardly say; but, taking a glass I saw two specks on a distant bluff which I believed to be Indians. I told White what I thought, and he stood guard while I ran to secure some of the meat, which I was determined to have. I cut away a tongue and tenderloin, and hurrying back, found the two specks had disappeared. This convinced me I was right, and we hastened to join the command. They had moved some distance, but, mounting a hill, we caught sight of the column and made for it with all speed. An officer, who like ourselves, had been some distance from the column saw two Indians riding about. If we had fired upon them when we saw them we would only be blamed for disturbing friendly Indians or frightening hostiles away; so we couldn't do anything. The Indians, when they arrived at Wolf's Point, were well armed, but evidently short of ammunition. They were refused any supplies, and said they would go where they could get them. A Sioux agent who visited their camp on Porcupine Creek, not far from Wolf's point, reported them as very bold and impudent. They searched his belt for ammunition and offered to trade a pony for 100 rounds. They further promised to return in the spring, when they would have fresh supplies, and fight the soldiers "plenty." They carried with them a number of cavalry pistols, such as were used by Custer's men, and which they were anxious to trade off, as they had no ammunition for them.

The following incident will show how bold and suspicious they are: A white man, who was taking one of the pistols in exchange for a coat, accidentally pointed it at the Indian with whom he was making the exchange. On the instant, two rifles were pointed upon him and only removed when the mistake was explained.

Our troops were now out of rations, but Terry arrived by boat with supplies and ordered Reno to return by the opposite bank of the river to Buford. The campaign was evidently over for the season, and General Terry and staff and myself returned by boat. From Buford we came to Bismark, the troops following by land. None of us could comprehend the meaning of any of the movements we made, and everything was kept very secret. It is the first compaign in which I could not understand any of the movements. Perhaps if I knew the object, that might explain them, but as it was, the Indians might have roamed around for twenty years and lived comfortably. The army made no use of their scouts. While among the Indians, spies were watching us from every hill top, and were in no danger of being caught.

WHEREABOUTS OF SITTING BULL

From all I can learn I believe Sitting Bull, with the main body of the hostile Sioux, is now in the vicinity of, or on the Little Missouri, hunting there. They are seeking winter supplies, and their tactics are evidently to avoid punishment. If they are followed by the soldiers their plan is to separate into small parties and spread or entirely destroy the trail, having previously agreed on a place of meeting. I don't think they want to renew the fight next spring. They are well aware that the soldiers will come well supplied and better prepared in every way to conduct a campaign. Their object is some peace policy which they hope to negotiate during the winter. They might refuse for some time to give up their arms and ponies, and a few bands might fight it out, but they could be easily annihilated.

A BIOGRAPHY OF SITTING BULL

Sitting Bull is an Hunkpapa Sioux, whose parentage on his father's side is altogether obscure, even among his own people. For this reason Sitting Bull was kicked and cuffed around when very young and badly treated by his youthful companions. It made him a fierce, bad Indian, and at ten years of age he took to the warpath. Before he was fifteen he ranked as a warrior among the tribe and was considered a dangerous enemy. In one of his early campaigns he captured a boy from another tribe, and in order to save his life he adopted him as a brother. This brother it was who came to the Hunkpapas and reported that Sitting Bull had asked to be considered as one of their people, as he had nothing more to keep him with the hostiles. This is very probably the origin of the story of his death, which I do not by any means think likely.

Mr. Omohundro does not expect to remain East long, but will return to the frontier. During the fall he will visit Colorado with a party of English sportsmen. He reports a great plenty of deer, antelope and buffalo on his last trip, and, having plenty of chances to hunt had fresh meat daily.

The last paragraph mentions a hunt with a party of English sportsmen. At the head of this group was Sir John Reid who had previously arranged with Texas Jack to act as guide for their hunt. It is of interest to note that whenever possible the English hunters always sought out Texas Jack as a guide for their parties, a fitting compliment to his ability as guide. All that is known of the results of this particular hunt is to be found in a Philadelphia newspaper of the time:[4]

TEXAS JACK'S FEAST

Grand Antelope Dinner and Speech by
"Arizona John" (John M. Burke)

On last Saturday evening a festive party sat down to a superb antelope dinner, given by J. B. Omohundro, better known as "Texas Jack," the well-known western scout and husband of Morlacchi, the celebrated danseuse, at Nash's Restaurant, on Chestnut Street, below Eleventh. Guests from New York and other widely scattered places were present. All this was to celebrate a very successful big game hunting trip to the wilds of the far West when Texas Jack was guide for Sir John Reid

[4] "The Omohundro Genealogical Record."

and a party of English sportsmen. The trip was exceedingly successful; and after taking Sir John's trophies of the hunt to New York for shipment to England, Texas Jack returned to this city, bringing with him a fine antelope and a magnificent deer which formed the staple of last evening's dinner.

According to Texas Jack's brother, the noted scout was at one time a guide for Lord Beckingham and a party of sportsmen. They were hunting grizzly bears in the Rocky Mountains. So well pleased was the English Lord with Jack's services that upon his return to England, he sent him a silver mounted rifle of considerable value, as a token of his appreciation.

Smithsonian Institute

BAPTISTE BAYHYLLE

A print from the original glass negative of this noted U. S. interpreter who was called La-shara-se-re-ter-rek or "One whom the great spirit smiles upon." He and Texas Jack were warm friends.

10

A DISTINGUISHED COUPLE

Accompanied by a splendid artist's sketch of the scout, the following article is one of the finest informal interviews with Texas Jack and his wife ever to be found. It reflects considerable new light on the lives of these two celebrated individuals.

A CHAT WITH TEXAS JACK.

The other evening, a little group sat in one of the parlors of the Hermann House, Bowery. It consisted of Texas Jack, Signora Morlacchi, his wife, Mr. Bell, our artist, and Critic.

Mr. Bell sketched, Texas Jack and the Signora chatted, whilst Critic listened and questioned.

John B. Omohundro, better known as Texas Jack, is one of the best types of an American loveable. Our friends, the Parisians, should see

The Signora.—Yes, I did once dance at that theatre, but I am not the Morlacchi I'm often mistaken for.

Critic.—I heard you sing remarkably well last night. [In her play of Thrice Married, the Signora sings *Ernani, Ernani, involami,* in a very artistic manner.]

The Signora, who is a remarkably pretty black-eyed Italian lady, with charming manners, answered, Yes, but I ought to sing better than I do. Signor Arditi, of Her Majesty's Theatre, London, wanted me to become a

When I was with the Earl of Dunraven we shot several huge grizzl bears.

Critic.—You were, then, out in the Yellowstone.

Texas Jack.—Yes, and a queer region it is. I can't attempt to describe it. It is all red, pink, blue, and yellow, odd rocks, and hot water spring There's one spot so weird and unnatural looking that they call it th Devil's Home, and the Indians declare bad spirits live in it. Near ther is a pyramid seventy feet high, evidently formed by a water-spout.

ARTIST'S SKETCH OF TEXAS JACK, 1877

While being interviewed by a reporter of *Spirit of the Times*, Texas Jack posed for this interesting sketch by the magazine's staff artist.

A CHAT WITH TEXAS JACK [1]

The other evening, a little group sat in one of the parlors of Hertmann House, Bowery. It consisted of Texas Jack, Signora Morlacchi, his wife, Mr. Bell, our artist, and Critic.

Mr. Bell sketched; Texas Jack and the Signora chatted, whilst Critic listened and questioned.

John B. Omohundro, better known as Texas Jack, is one of the best types of an American imaginable. Our friends, the Parisians, should see Jack, and their opinions of our men would be considerably modified. Here is a man old Dumas would have immortalized, and Ponson du Terrail made the hero of a series of novels in fifty-eight volumes.

Texas Jack has a novel and most sympathetic face, beaming with intelligence and kindliness. The peculiarities of two great races are easily traced in its features. The regular and beautiful aquiline profile is French, Norman. His mother was a French lady, and he tells us, reputed to be a most lovely woman. She died when he was young, hence he does not speak her language. She had seven sons, Texas Jack is the lowest in stature, being exactly six feet high. If you are well acquainted with the portraits of courtiers of the time of Louis XIV, which the brush of Phillipe de Champagne has left in the galleries of Paris, you will at once recognize, when you see Jack, that he possesses the finest type of French face. But in the exceeding breadth of the cheek bones, the peculiar oval of the forehead, and the firmness and power of the jaw, it is evident that he has Indian ancestors. His father comes of a grand tribe, the Powhattan, to which belonged the famous heroine Pocahontas.

"I've seen my uncles on my father's side," said he. "They were all men over six feet; Indeed I am the shortest of the family. It appears we degenerate in stature. My grandfather and his people were all of them six feet two and three inches. My father and his brothers were not so tall, and, although I'm six feet, and my brothers are still taller, yet none of them reach six feet two inches. It is so with all Indian families; civilization does not seem to agree with them."

Critic—"What do you think will be the end of the American Indians?"

Texas Jack—"They'll all be swept away, except the Cherokees. That tribe intermarries with the whites, gets civilized, and forms the finest race of men and women in the world."

Critic—"You have very little faith in the Western Indians?"

[1] *Spirit of the Times*, April 14, 1877.

Texas Jack—"Very little. They are so inferior to the East-erns that I imagine in a hundred years or so, they will be quite extinct. You see the best Western Indians are the few who were driven from these States by the advance of civilization."

Critic—"Do you speak any of their languages?"

Texas Jack—"Oh, dear, yes, several. But they are really not beautiful; the perpetual recurrence of the *chi* and *cha* make them sound like chatterings."

Critic—"But they are very rich in words, are they not?"

Texas Jack—"By no means, they are quite the contrary, very poor. They possess few words, and all these words have double, and even treble, and quite opposite meanings. Hence when they are translated they have such a grandiloquent sound. I fancy the dialects of the Eastern Indians were finer than the Western, but so much is exaggerated concerning them that to read of their speeches you would think they were so many Miltons; but, I assure you, they talk very common-place talk, and display their ignorance at every turn."

Critic—"Do you recognize French or English words amongst their's?"

Texas Jack—"Occasionally, and even Italian and Spanish, but these were doubtless introduced by the missionaries, and, chiefly apply to articles of furniture and agriculture, borrowed from us. They also have words that sound just like English, but have a very different meaning; thus, heart means tongue, and dart, eye. My opinion of their language is not a high one at all. Indeed they are so poor that pantomime is absolutely necessary in order to supply the want of words and sentences."

Critic—"What do you think of the intelligence of the Indians?"

Texas Jack—"Some tribes are very clever and sharp. All Indians have marked peculiarities, which are interesting. Nearly all of them are great physiognomists, and can determine your character by your face, and this with surprising ease. I inherit this."

(Here a request was made by the artist, who was taking the portrait which heads this article, for silence, and Mr. Jack relapsed into quietude. Meanwhile Critic attacked the Signora, and a lively conversation ensued.)

The Signora—"I have been married four years to Mr. Omohun-dro, but it seems to me as if I had known him all my life. He is very good and kind, and never angry. No, I have not yet accompanied him on any of his expeditions into the prairies. He always leaves me at home, but I want to go, and shall, I

hope, be of the next party. I suppose, however, I shall have
to be left somewhere on the confines of civilization. Still, I am
strong, and do not mind fatigue, though I strongly object to
bears and rattlesnakes."

Critic—"You used to dance at the Scala, at Milan, did you
not?"

The Signora—"Yes, I did once dance at that theater, but I
am not the Morlacchi I'm often mistaken for."

Critic—"I heard you sing remarkably well last night. (In her
play of *Thrice Married*, the Signora sings *Ernani, Ernani, in-
volarmi*, in a very artistic manner.)

The Signora, who is a remarkably pretty black-eyed Italian
lady, with charming manners, answered, "Yes but I ought to
sing better than I do. Signor Arditi, of Her Majesty's Theatre,
London, wanted me to become a singer, but I preferred my
dancing. I have a strong, dramatic, soprano voice, in the style
of Mlle. Titiens, but I never cultivated it to any great extent.
I can get along without Norma of Lucrezia. My husband can
act also very well. You see he belongs to the Indian race, which
pantomimes wonderfully, and also to the French, who are born
actors. You will scarcely believe me when I tell you that he
can act Quasimodo to perfection, although he won't play it in
public. He cripples himself up to look like a hunchback, and
it is a capital performance."

Critic—"We can ill imagine such a superb man acting the role
of a hunchback."

The Signora—"Well, he can do it. I have played Esmeralda
all over the country, but never with him."

By this time Texas Jack was allowed to talk again, and we
began conversing about pantomiming. A gentleman, who is well
acquainted with the Italian style of pantomime, now joined us,
and began to pantomime with the famous scout. "Ah! you are
like my wife," cried he, "you can only do the broad and decided
gestures, but I can achieve something far more subtle. Now
watch, I will repeat in pantomime anything you wish me to
say to yonder Indian." He pointed to an Indian of his company
seated at the other end of the room, and both fell to talking
by gestures so slight, and yet so expressive, that a long conversation was held by these means, which was afterward interpreted to us. "Now, you Italian and French people cannot do
that sort of thing. You must have Indian blood in you to do it.
You can only express broad passions and feelings. We can speak.
Even my wife, a pantomimist by profession, and an Italian to
boot, cannot do what we do. Now I will read your character

and tell you the impression you made upon me at first sight, and afterward you will confess to me if I am right or wrong, and pardon me if I wound you, but remember it is your own wish to know, and so you shall."

Texas Jack then told to us each our character, in so surprisingly truthful a manner, that it seemed supernatural. "That is another Indian gift, and a very necessary one to us who have to roam the plains amongst all kinds of dangerous men. Think of the life I've led! I am a link between civilization and the other thing. I have to endure hardships, live amongst renegades and savages, and this is the kind of life my ancestors led for countless generations before me. Do you wonder if I possess, by inheritance and habit, some peculiar gifts indispensable to a man in my position?"

Critic—"Do all Indians have these faculties?"

Texas Jack—"In a more or less degree. Of course they don't all of them understand the traits of the civilized men as well as I do, and, therefore, are sometimes mistaken."

Critic—"Do you like acting?"

Texas Jack—"Yes, but I can scarcely call acting the performances I give. They, however, suit my public and purpose by giving folks some idea of savage life. I think I could act very well, and my wife, a fine artiste, thinks so too."

Critic—"The Signora is an artiste of a very versatile kind, and a very charming one. You could have no better professor in the art."

Texas Jack—"I'm glad you think so, for she is really a very superior woman. I first acted in Chicago, but have not much experience in the profession even now. I like the plains, and my life there best; I'm going out again soon with an English Captain. You know I was with Earl Dunraven some time ago."

Critic—"Did you like him?"

Texas Jack—"Very much, indeed. He is a perfect gentleman, highly cultivated, and most amiable. I enjoyed the trip with him. He is so much of a man."

Critic—"The scenery in the Far West must be wonderful."

Texas Jack—"Beyond all power of description, grand and strange. You cannot imagine what it is like. The Yellowstone region is far more beautiful than any fairy scene in your plays here. The coloring is so vivid and surprising, that if you did not see it you would not believe it possible. The Yellowstone is one of the wonders of the earth, but there are other like places out there quite as interesting."

Critic—"I suppose civilization is getting along even there, and changing things greatly."

Texas Jack—"One thing to be observed is that civilization has plenty of room to stir about in there, and I guess it will take a long time to upset things generally. Some one told me that buffaloes were already decreasing. I don't believe it. I saw last season, herds of many thousands dashing along the prairies. The bears may diminish, by going higher up into the hills, and the snakes might, with advantage, disappear altogether. When I was with the Earl of Dunraven we shot several hugh grizzly bears."

Critic—"You were, then, out in the Yellowstone?"

Texas Jack—"Yes, and a queer region it is. I can't attempt to describe it. It is all red, pink, blue, and yellow, odd rocks, and hot water springs. There's one spot so weird and unnatural looking that they call it the Devil's Home, and the Indians declare bad spirits live in it. Near there is a pyramid seventy feet high, evidently formed by a waterspout. It stands on a level, is small at both ends, and large in the middle. It is perfectly dry, and looks somewhat like a ram standing on its head. I left my lariat one night in one of the Geyser springs, and, lo! the next day I found it turned to stone. A man would be petrified in the same way, if he remained long enough in the water. The Tower Falls in the Yellowstone are splendid, over two hundred feet high, but the Grand Fall is far finer. It rushes over five hundred feet of rock. Imagine, we found a lake, twenty yards in circumference, of boiling water, and smelling like scalded pigs. Thousands of tons of water were hurled up from its centre, to thirty and forty feet, in lofty spouts. There is little or no vegetation, and, of course, little or no animal life in this terrible and fantastic region. It is so strange that I advise anyone to go and see it, for if anyone tells them about it, they will barely believe what they hear."

Critic—"Is it finer than the Yosemite?"

Texas Jack—"It is nothing like as beautiful. Yosemite is lovely. The Yellowstone is queer, but both are very well worth the trouble of being visited. Earl Dunraven's book, The Great Divide, gives a splendid description of the place, and I can assure you the Earl deserves a high compliment on that work, which you should read. Sir John Reid and his cousin Eaton are very accomplished men, and I enjoyed being with them. They are first rate hunters. English gentlemen of their class give a fine example of manliness by the way they come out and hunt, and discover things in the unknown parts of our continent. They bring education and science with them. I have been with several who were scientists, botanists, and naturalists of high order, as well as huntsmen."

Critic—"In your last letter to THE SPIRIT you mentioned Florida. Do you like that country?"

Texas Jack—"Yes, very much, but it is the climate which makes its chief charm. It is very mild, and yet not enervating. Hunting down there is good, but it is the great Mexican and California range which is most worth seeing."

Here the Signora rose to bid us farewell, and after a few compliments to that lovely and accomplished young lady, we were obliged, much against our will, to take leave of her gallant husband. We say "much against our will," because so fascinating is the conversation of this distinguished huntsman that it is difficult to imagine any more delightful manner of passing the time than in the company of one whose experience is so vast, and whose observation is so just and intelligent.

It was not strange that stories of the exploits of this quiet, unassuming buckskin-clad scout would reach the ears of writers of a certain type of sensational fiction, which was then much in vogue. The outcome of hearing such reports on the noted plainsman are recounted in the next chapter.

Mlle. Morlacchi and Mlle. Baretta while with DePol's Ballet Troupe.

11

HERO OF THE DIME NOVELS

THE middle seventies saw the heyday of a
unique type of literature on the American
scene. True, there had been earlier paper backed novels of a
sensational nature. But it remained for the "Dime Novels" to
usher in a new era for readers of the blood and thunder type
of writing, which included such lurid descriptions as:

I'm Mustang Sam, the high muck-a-muck of E. Pluribus Unum!
I was got by a bull whale out o' a iceberg. I kin yell louder,
run furder, ride faster, shoot straighter, jump higher, tell bigger
lies, eat more bull an' jump outside o' more chained lightnin'
then any other two-legged critter as was ever pupped. I'm the
man that swum the Big Kenyon of the Colorado on my back.
I'm the critter what climbed up a greased rainbow an' bit the
highest p'int off o' the new moon. I'm Mustang Sam—how goes
it, stranger? [1]

Published mostly in small convenient formats, these in-
struments of written sensationalism found a ready market
among certain segments of the reading public. It is said the
Dime Novels did more to while away lazy summer afternoons
in the hayloft than all of the works of Shakespeare, Dickens
or Scott combined.

Fictitious for the most part, many of them, nevertheless,
did have a thread of fact running through the adventurous
and sensational stories which were found between their lurid
paper covers. Strictly speaking, a Dime Novel was a small
paper pamphlet containing a complete novel. Many times
they sold for a nickel rather than a dime, and, some were of
a larger, weekly type format, but in common parlance they
were all "Dime Novels."

One requirement had to be met by those which would be
the most successful. With all their hair raising fictional experi-

---

[1] John E. Badger in "Mustang Sam; or, The King of the Plains."

ences, there must be also a reasonableness to the situations to satisfy those who were familiar with life in the West. This is probably the primary reason for the success of the dime novelist Ned Buntline. Not only had he been a sort of "soldier of fortune," but he had also traveled in the West enough to get on to many of the colloquialisms and customs of frontier life.

It was on one of these trips that he made the acquaintance of and formed a friendship with Texas Jack. In all probability it was at the same time as his first meeting with Buffalo Bill at Fort McPherson, but whenever it was, he must have been much impressed with the western scout. It was not long after this that his first novel with Texas Jack as the hero was written.

Buntline introduced the youthful scout to his reading public with the following wording, which is taken from chapter three of "TEXAS JACK the White King of the Pawnees."

"Trailed—and by a hundred of the fiends! Now, good angels, help me!"

This was the utterance of a young man, nobly formed, clad in the picturesque buckskin garb worn by the hunter scouts of the far West, armed with knife, revolver, and rifle, and mounted on a splendid horse of the mixed American and mustang stock.

He had just risen to the crest of a sandy ridge near the base of the famous Black Hills, and looking back he saw a large body of Indians riding in column, swiftly along the very route by which he had come. They were on his track.

"If I had but fifty of my brave Pawnees, I would not turn my back on a hundred of these cowardly Sioux. But alone there is no show to fight till I'm cornered. Then it will be fight and die! Forward Duke! It is your speed alone which can get me, out of this scrape. There is cover, but it is twenty miles ahead. Go, my good horse—go, for the red devils see us!"

The horse responded nobly to the touch of his master's heel, and sped on at a gait which showed a gain upon the red pursuers when the hunter next looked back.

But as wolves follow the deer, so the red fiends kept on tirelessly, and when full half the distance to the treecrowned hills was done, more than half of them were yet nearer than when the white rider first discovered them.

NEW YORK WEEKLY, MARCH 24, 1873

Featuring the first installment of "Texas Jack . . . The white King of the Pawnees," by Ned Buntline. This serial made its appearance at the same time that Texas Jack was on the stage with Buffalo Bill in *The Scouts of the Prairie*. The striking portrait of Jack was used on posters advertising the show.

G. A. Custer
GENERAL

D. L. Payne
CAPT. PAYNE
"The Cimarron Scout"

D. Frank Powell.
"WHITE BEAVER"

P. H. Sheridan
GENERAL

J. W. Crawford
"CAPT. JACK"
"The Poet Scout"

G. W. Lillie
"PAWNEE BILL"

J. J. Reynolds
GENERAL

W. F. Carver
"DOC CARVER"

Nelson A. Miles
GENERAL

John M. Burke
"ARIZONA JOHN"

Dr. Richard Tanner
"DIAMOND DICK"

L. H. North
CAPTAIN

George Crook
GENERAL

R. W. Clarke
"DEADWOOD DICK"

Frank North
MAJOR

PROMINENT NAMES OF THE OLD WEST

Most of the men represented by these signatures were close friends or acquaintances of Texas Jack during the years he was a scout and guide on the plains.

JACK HOLDING THE INDIANS AT BAY

Taken from Buel's book *"Heroes of the Plains"* this artist's sketch is typical of the early wood-engraved illustrations. It depicts an event in the life of Texas Jack while on the cattle ranches of Texas.

Nearer and nearer to the hills, the trees rising at every leap of the faithful horse; but nearer, too, the bloodhounds in the rear.

The rider in advance, who had looked back but little in the start, now kept an almost constant eye over his shoulder.

"They think they have me!" he muttered. "If they have they'll find me a hard nut to crack. More than one yelling devil will eat lead for his supper before I go under. On-on, good Duke! We may beat 'em yet!"

The horse, apparently cheered by his master's voice, gave a few mighty bounds, and the latter, surprised and rejoicing, thinking he would surely gain the hills in advance of the red fiends, shouted out a wild defiance to the demons of the plains.

Alas! Like many a triumph, his seemed short-lived, for the horse suddenly fell to the earth, and, with a groan as if its heart had burst, quivered in the death-agony.

The bold rider did not flinch. As the horse staggered and fell, the former left his stirrups and stood firmly upon the ground, facing the coming foe as cooly as if ten thousand men were at his back.

"Come, you red fiends, come!" he said, bitterly. "Yell your loudest while you can, for more than one will yell his last ere Texas Jack goes under!"

Col. Judson's (Ned Buntline) own comment regarding the serial is contained in this letter taken from the Jan. 6, 1873 issue of the *New York Weekly.*

MESSRS. STREET AND SMITH, In furnishing to you the last page of MSS., it rejoices me to say, that in this story, "Texas Jack," I have given you the crowning effort of all my Western Series of Life-Pictures.

Whether it is because I have had so much of the real History of the great original hero in my hands, or because I love him and his mate Buffalo Bill as if they were my own brothers, that I have succeeded so well, I cannot say. But I do say, and I know that your millions of intelligent readers will also say, that this *is* my VERY BEST story.

Yours Truly,
EDWARD Z. C. Judson ("Ned Buntline")

Eagle Lodge, in the Pines, Nov., 1872

"TEXAS JACK, The White King of the Pawnees" first appeared in Street and Smith's *New York Weekly* Vol. XXVIII, No. 20, under the date of March 24, 1873. It ran as a serial up to and including issue No. 33, June 23, 1873. It may have been Buntline's attempt to establish Texas Jack nationally as he had done with Buffalo Bill in *Buffalo Bill The King of Border Men* some two years before. In any event the serial, which ran during the time the play, *The Scouts of the Prairie*, was on the road, was eagerly received. It was the forerunner of many more novels in which Texas Jack played the part of the hero or one of the prominent characters. This first thrilling story of Texas Jack's frontier life proved to be most popular with readers and was reprinted at various times in the following Street and Smith Publications:

New York Weekly ...reprinted again as a serial in 1887
Sea and Shore Series No. 28 1891
Log Cabin Library No. 132 1891
Log Cabin Pocket Edition No. 31 1898
Log Cabin Pocket Edition No. 169 1901

Some years after this, Buntline produced another novel with Texas Jack as the hero. This one, "TEXAS JACK'S CHUMS, or The Whirlwind of the West" appeared in No. 316, *Nickel Library*, 1883.

One of the most prolific and best known of all Dime Novel authors was Col. Prentiss Ingraham. It is said that nearly a thousand novels came from his pen in his almost thirty-four years of writing. Like Buntline he was a veritable soldier of fortune, having traveled in many foreign countries, fought in several wars and had lived in the West for a while where he became acquainted with many of the frontier scouts.

Ingraham's novel, "TEXAS JACK, The Mustang King," first appeared in the quarto edition of the *Beadle's Boys Library*, No. 5, of January 11, 1882. Two years later it was used in the *Beadle's Boys Library*, Octavo Edition, No. 10, June 21, 1884. The last reprint of this sensational story concerning Texas Jack made its appearance in the *Beadle's Pocket Library*, No. 392, July 15, 1891.

Col. Ingraham used several *nom de plumes* in his writing. It is said that he wrote some of the novels credited to Buffalo Bill after that scout grew tired of writing. The Novel, "NED WYLDE, The Boy Scout," by "Texas Jack" (J. B. Omohundro) is generally credited to Ingraham. This novel first appeared in serial form in *The Saturday Journal* Vol. VII, beginning with No. 348, November 11, 1876 and ending in No. 354, December 23, 1876. Some years later it came out in novel form in *Beadle's Half Dime Pocket Library*, Third Edition, Vol. 1, No. 9, March 19, 1884. It was reprinted again in No. 1059 of the same series and in *Beadle's Half Dime Library* No. 38.

Wm. F. Cody ("Buffalo Bill") also authored a couple of novels about his old "pard," Texas Jack. The first "Texas Jack, the Prairie Rattler; or, The Queen of the Wild Horses," was written as a serial for *Beadle's Weekly*. It began in issue No. 40, (August 18, 1883) and ran to issue No. 50 (Oct. 27, 1883). His second, "TEXAS JACK, The Lasso King; or, The Robber Rangers of the Rio Grande," was likewise a serial. It began in issue No. 615 (August 25, 1894) of *The Banner Weekly*, and ended in No. 627, (November 17, 1894). In 1897 it was reprinted in the No. 969 issue of *Beadle's Dime Library*.

One of the earlier novels about Texas Jack is the one written by someone using the pseudonym of "Lone Star" and

DIME NOVELS

Covers from four of the better known Dime Novels and weekly papers
in which Texas Jack was the hero.

No. 969. Published Every Wednesday. Beadle & Adams, Publishers, 98 WILLIAM STREET, NEW YORK. Ten Cents a Copy. $5.00 a Year. Vol. LXXV.

TEXAS JACK,

THE LASSO KING;
OR,
The Robber Rangers of the Rio Grande.

TEXAS JACK IN THE LEAD, RIDING LIKE A VERITABLE CENTAUR—A COMMANDING AND NOBLE FIGURE.

Vol. XXIV. Published Every Wednesday. Beadle & Adams, Publishers, 98 WILLIAM STREET, N. Y., August 26, 1884. Ten Cents a Copy. $5.00 a Year! No. 304.

TEXAS JACK,
THE PRAIRIE RATTLER; or, THE QUEEN OF THE WILD RIDERS.

A Romance in the Life of a Real Hero—John B. Omohundro—Texas Jack—and a Tale of the Southwest Border.

BY HON. WM. F. CODY—"Buffalo Bill,"

AUTHOR OF "THE GOLD BULLET SPORT," "KANSAS KING," "DEADLY EYE," "THE PRAIRIE SPY," ETC., ETC.

"YES, IT IS MY LOVELY ZEPA THAT IS COMING BACK TO ME, AND BY HER SIDE RIDES THAT PRINCE OF TEXANS, WHOM MEN CALL THE THUNDERBOLT."

Copyrighted, 1884, by Beadle and Adams. Entered at the Post Office at New York, N.Y., as Second Class Mail Matter. Mar. 18, 1886.

Vol. I. $2.50 a Year. Published Weekly by Beadle and Adams, No. 98 WILLIAM ST., New York. Price, Five Cents. No. 9.

NED WYLDE, The Boy Scout. BY "TEXAS JACK,"
(J. B. Omohundro.)

CHAPTER I.
THE GRAVE IN THE COTTONWOOD.

A Boy lay fast asleep beneath the shelter of three cottonwoods. The hour was bordering upon midnight, and he slept soundly, as though worn out with a long tramp—a weary tracking of a faint trail leading toward the Big Horn Mountains—the Switzerland of the mighty West.

His garments were worn and travel-stained, and his face and hands browned by exposure to wind, and rain and sun.

Suddenly the sleeper awoke with a slight start, as though some grim

TEXAS JACK.

Copyrighted, 1887, by Beadle and Adams. Entered as Second Class Matter at the New York, N.Y., Post Office. July 13, 1881.

No. 392. $2.50 a Year. Published Weekly by Beadle and Adams, No. 98 WILLIAM ST. New York. Price, Five Cents. Vol. XXXI.

TEXAS JACK

THE MUSTANG KING.

Covers of four of the celebrated Beadle Dimé Novels featuring Texas Jack.

entitled "TEXAS JACK." It appeared in 1872 in issue No. 102 of *DeWitt's Ten Cent Romances.*

In addition to these which featured Texas Jack in the main title, there are to be found many in which he is listed in the sub title. A few such, taken from Albert Johannsen's monumental work entitled "The House of Beadle and Adams," [2] and published by the University of Oklahoma Press, are listed here:

"Buffalo Bill's Flush Hand; or TEXAS JACK'S BRAVOS" by Prentiss Ingraham, *Beadle's Dime Library,* No. 743 (Jan. 18, 1893).

"The Wild Steer Riders; or, TEXAS JACK'S TERRORS" by Prentiss Ingraham, Banner's Weekly No. 347 Vol. VII, No. 347 (July 6, 1899) to VII, No. 359 (Sept. 28, 1889) and *Beadle's Dime Library,* No. 834 (Oct. 17, 1894).

"The Ranch King Deadshot; or, TEXAS JACK'S PROXY" by Wm. F. Cody, *Beadle's Dime Library* No. 839 (Nov. 21, 1894).

"Buffalo Bill's Red Skin Ruse; or, TEXAS JACK'S DEAD SHOT" by Prentiss Ingraham, *Beadle's Dime Library* No. 845 (Jan. 2, 1895).

"Buffalo Bill's Rough Riders; or, TEXAS JACK'S SHARP-SHOOTERS" by Prentiss Ingraham, *Beadle's Dime Library* No. 900 (Jan. 22, 1896).

"Arizona Joe—the Boy Pard of TEXAS JACK. A story of the Strange Life of Captain Joe Bruce, a Young Scout, Indian Fighter, Miner and Ranger, and a Protege of J. B. Omohundro, the Famous Texas Jack," by Prentiss Ingraham, *Beadle's Half Dime Library* No. 495 (January 18, 1887).

In many of the novels in which Buffalo Bill was featured as the hero, his pard, Texas Jack, also played an important role, even though not listed in the subtitle. Representative titles under this classification are as follows:

"The Dead Shot Nine; or, My Pards on the Plains," by Wm. F. Cody, *Beadle's Dime Library* No. 599 (April 16, 1890).

"Buffalo Bill Baffled; or, The Deserter Desperado's Defiance" by Prentiss Ingraham, *Beadle's Dime Library* No. 710 (June 1, 1892), New Mexico, Indian country, Fort Beau-

---

[2] Used by special permission of the University of Oklahoma Press, Norman, Okla.

Advertisement from the *New York Weekly*,
issue of Feb. 24, 1873.

vior. A story featuring Cody, Powell, Omohundro, and others.

"Buffalo Bill's Body-Guard; or, The Still Hunt of the Hills. The Story of the 'Robber of the Ranges'," by Prentiss Ingraham, *Beadle's Dime Library* No. 727 (September 28, 1892). A Silk Lasso Sam story, with Buffalo Bill, Texas Jack, and Dr. Powell taking part.

"Buffalo Bill's Beagles; or, Silk Lasso Sam, the Outlaw of the Overland. A Story of Wild West Heroes and Heroism," by Prentiss Ingraham, *Beadle's Dime Library* No. 731 (Oct. 26, 1892). Buffalo Bill, Texas Jack, Dr. Powell and others are the leading characters.

"Buffalo Bill and His Merry Men," by Prentiss Ingraham, *Beadle's Dime Library* No. 735 (November 23, 1892). Buffalo Bill, Texas Jack, Wild Bill and Dr. Powell are the heroes.

"Buffalo Bill's Tangled Trail; or, Gentleman Jack, the Man of Many Masks. A Romance of Tangled Trails Followed by Buffalo Bill and His Buckskin Heroes, Surgeon Frank Powell, Wild Bill, Texas Jack, Captain Jack Crawford, Buckskin Sam, Colorado Carl, and a Mysterious Unknown," by Prentiss Ingraham, *Beadle's Dime Library* No. 904 (February 19, 1896).

"Buffalo Bill at Bay; or, The Gold-Seeker's Doom. A Story of the Great Scout's Red Ally," by Prentiss Ingraham, *Beadle's Dime Library* No. 950 (January 6, 1897). Lost in a blizzard. Buffalo Bill, General Miles, Texas Jack, and Dr. Powell take part.

"The Dead Shot Four; or, My Pards of the Plains. A Romance of Wild Careers and Heroic Manhood in Dark Days Camp," by William F. Cody, *Beadle's Dime Library* No. 973 (June 16, 1897) *Banner Weekly* No. 752 (April 10, 1897) "Dark Days," a mining camp out West. Texas Jack, Wild Bill, the Powells, and Buffalo Bill have parts in the story.

"Buffalo Bill's Relentless Trail; or, The Unknown Slayer of the Black Cavalry," by Prentiss Ingraham, *Beadle's Dime Library* No. 979 (July 28, 1897) Arizona Territory, Buffalo Bill, Wild Bill, Dr. Powell and Texas Jack perform wonders.

The following list, with but one exception all appeared in *The Banner Weekly*. The first one listed is from *Beadle's Weekly*.

The Banner Weekly to the Front!   With Change of Title we give this Great Banner Story!

THE Banner Weekly

Vol. IV.   NEW YORK, NOVEMBER 14, 1885.   No. 157

THE DEAD SHOT NINE;

Or, MY PARDS OF THE PLAINS.

BY HON. WM. F. CODY, "Buffalo Bill."

Texas Jack is featured in this story by Buffalo Bill along with other
frontier characters of the time.

"The League of Three; or, Buffalo Bill's Pledge," by Prentiss Ingraham, No. 1 (Nov. 18, 1882), to No. 13 (Feb. 10, 1883). A story of a trail followed to the bitter end by the three famous scouts, Buffalo Bill, Wild Bill and Texas Jack.

"The Dead-shot Nine; or, My Pards of the Plains," by William F. Cody, Vol. IV, No. 157 (Nov. 14, 1885), to Vol. 169 (Feb. 6, 1886). Kansas in the 1870's. Getting after the "Red Owl" gang. Cody, Wild Bill, Texas Jack and Dr. Frank Powell take part.

"The Wild Steer Riders; or, The Red Revolver Rangers," by Prentiss Ingraham, Vol. VII, No. 347 (July 6, 1889, to No. 359 (Sept. 28, 1889). Baltimore and Texas—Indians, gamblers, card sharks; cowboys: Texas Jack, Buck Taylor, Buckskin Sam, etc.

"Buffalo Bill's Brand; or, The Brimstone Brotherhood," by Prentiss Ingraham, Vol. VII, No. 359 (Sept. 28, 1889, to Vol. VIII, No. 371 (Dec. 21, 1889). A romance of Army—, Scout and Wild Life in the True Wild West. Fort Fairview with Buffalo Bill, Texas Jack and Dr. Powell.

"Buffalo Bill's Boys in Blue; or, The Officer Outcast," by Prentiss Ingraham, Vol. VIII, No. 371 (Dec. 21, 1889), to No. 383 (March 15, 1890). Valley City on the Overland Trail. She sold herself for her lover's life—Cody, Powell and Texas Jack are featured.

"Buffalo Bill's Buckskin Braves; or, The Renegade Queen" by Prentiss Ingraham, Vol. VIII, No. 383 (March 15, 1890), to No. 395 (June 7, 1890). A Romance of Life in the Wild West—with Buffalo Bill, Dr. Powell, Texas Jack, Sioux Indians, outlaws, soldiers and gamblers at "Fort Fairview and Gold Pocket."

"Gentleman Jack, the Man of Many Masks; or, Buffalo Bill's Peerless Pard," by Prentiss Ingraham, Vol. IX, No. 419 (Nov. 22, 1890), to No. 432 (Feb. 21, 1891). A Romance of Tangled Trails followed by Buffalo Bill and his Buckskin Heroes, Surgeon Frank Powell, Wild Bill, Texas Jack, Capt. Jack Crawford, Buckskin Sam, Colorado Carl and a Mysterious Unknown.

"Red Butterfly, the Spy of the Overland; or, The Nine Scouts League," by Prentiss Ingraham, Vol. IX, No. 431 (Feb. 14, 1891), to Vol. IX, No. 443 (May 9, 1891). Colorado in the 1870's, also Lake George, N. Y. Quantrel's band, Buffalo Bill, Wild Bill, Texas Jack, the Powells, Capt. Jack

Go-Wan-Go, Indians, a ventriloquist and a ghostly stage coach.

Had not Texas Jack's untimely death prevented it, very likely he would have appeared as a hero in many, many more stories of the frontier. He was the type of plainsman that appealed to writers of western novels. Picturesque, daring, brave and resourceful, he was a credit to the Old West in which he spent some of the happiest years of his life. In his unobtrusive way he delighted in doing the tasks that proved too difficult for others, and yet in the performance of such deeds he unconsciously was doing the things which brought recognition and made him the ideal hero of the Dime Novels.

J. B. OMOHUNDRO (TEXAS JACK).

In the March 3, 1873 issue of the *New York Weekly* there appeared this note:—A likeness of Texas Jack . . . In the NEW YORK WEEKLY containing the opening chapters of Ned Buntline's last great story, "TEXAS JACK," which will be commenced very soon, we shall give an accurate likeness of the dashing hero, whose wonderful exploits are fully equal to those of his mate, the renowned Buffalo Bill. The picture is from a photograph, taken expressly for the purpose, and represents Texas Jack with the fidelity of a mirror.

12

JACK AND JOSEPHINE

THE HUMAN SIDE of these two young
people is nearly obscured by the brighter spotlight which had been turned upon their professional lives.
Drawing back the curtain of public acclaim, one discovers a
splendid young couple not too different from other young
people of the time. In a brief chapter then let us present
Josephine—the woman, and Jack—the man.

Josephine was educated in the culture and refinement of
the old world schools.[1] Small in stature she was endowed
with delicate and refined features. Much has been mentioned
about her warm blooded eyes—expressive eyes that gave a
hint of her vivacious Italian temperament.

Full of fun, always ready for a joke or prank, she seemed
never to have a dull moment. One account tells how while
at home in East Billerica she flabbergasted the neighbors one
day by driving down the street in a smart rig with her sister—
both of them dressed in male attire, top hats and all. The
incident was featured at the time in a cartoon with the
caption, "Billerica girls gaze in astonishment at Mlle. Morlacchi."[2]

In addition to her ability as a dancer and actress, she was
an astute business woman. At the age of twenty-three she was
managing her own ballet troupe and doing an excellent job of
it. She not only knew the value of her ability as a dancer,
but also how to capitalize upon it—a failing all too often of
so many talented people.

When off the stage and at home, she was ever a typical

---

[1] *Lowell Daily Citizen*, July 24, 1886.
[2] Correspondence with Dr. A. Warren Stearns.

little housewife, keeping the home attractive for the man she adored, doing little kindnesses for the neighbors, always ready to assist in any community project and to lend her talents for its success. The small children found in her a sympathetic and understanding friend. Having no children of her own, she responded to their childish admiration with whole-hearted enthusiasm. Small wonder that the citizens of the city she called home, took her so to their bosoms.

There was also a serious side to this adorable little creature. It would manifest itself when she felt anyone had been wronged unduly. Then she would appear in all her indignation as a champion of the underdog, causing the wrong doers to beat a hasty retreat. At the fatal illness of her gallant husband, she insisted on ministering to him with all the love and affection of a devoted wife—even to the point of total exhaustion. A few short years later, she gave months of unselfish care and attention to her sister Angelina during her last illness.

Raised in the Catholic faith, Josephine was a devout member of the Church until her death. She found much happiness in "doing unto others as you would they should do unto you." Even in her busy show-life she took time out to attend the services of her faith—in whatever city the troupe happened to find itself.

Something seemed to go out of her theatrical life with the passing of her plainsman-actor husband. For seven years they had been on the stage together and to continue it alone was more than she could stand. With money saved up from her acting, she retired to the only American home she knew— a home surrounded with memories of Jack and the happy times they had spent together.

All of these attributes plus a downright zest for living made her a favorite with all who knew her. It was a sad day for the entire community when the bells tolled of her untimely passing. Rich and poor, learned and unschooled alike mourned her—a fitting and splendid tribute to the little Italian born ballerina with the twinkling toes and flashing eyes.

The life of Texas Jack: scout, guide, Indian fighter, plainsman, cowboy, hunter and actor, looms so large that it is likely to overshadow Texas Jack, the man.

Texas Jack was no saint; neither was he a scoundrel. He was, above all, a man's man and a true exponent of the manhood of the Old West. He lived in an age that called for and demanded the best in those whose names would be emblazoned high on the roll of immortals of the plans. In none of these requirements was Texas Jack found wanting. He talked little of his own accomplishments, which were many and varied.

His loyalty to his friends, an unfaltering courage in line of duty and a resourcefulness under adverse situations were but a few of his many attributes. None ever questioned his honesty, and his word was as good as gold. He was ever ready to champion the helpless or willing to lend a hand to those less fortunate. He recognized the rights of others and respected those rights. He made friends easily and retained their friendship for life. Even the Indians against whom he fought found in him a staunch friend, when the fighting was over. They respected him for his sympathetic understanding of their problems.

Texas Jack was of a mild disposition, soft spoken, with a smile and joke for all. But woe be to him who excited his anger, for he was a dangerous adversary when aroused. He loved sports and social events. Mrs. Cody recalls that on numerous occasions, while living at Ft. McPherson, she had heard him call dances.

It is said of him that he was happiest when recounting some tale of adventure in the West to a group of boys and girls. His genial manner made him a favorite with the young people wherever he happened to be.[3] If nothing else was known of Texas Jack, this love of children would be sufficient to set him apart from the common crowd. He was not the type to "draw the long bow" in his story telling.

---

[3] *Lowell Daily Citizen*, July 24, 1886.

He had that rare faculty of delighting his listeners with actual happenings spiced with a soft southern humor which was so characteristic of him. And both kiddies and adults loved it.

His family life was one of true happiness. He and his lovely wife found enjoyment and contentment in each other's company. He was sympathetic when the stage called her to fill engagements over and beyond the season with his troupe. She, too, had an understanding heart when he became restless with a yen to tramp the plains as a scout or as a guide for hunting parties, during the idle months away from the theater.

His younger brother, Malvern H., recalled that Texas Jack wrote quite regularly to his father during the years he was away from the old home. What a pity those letters, in which many times he recounted extremely interesting experiences on the plains, were never preserved. They would have made a priceless contribution to the historical lore of the Old West. The fact of his keeping in touch with his father does indicate a close family bond between father and son. It is said that one of his father's delights was in telling friends and relatives of his noted son. His parental pride knew no bounds when some new recognition came to "his boy" out on the western plains.

In appearance Texas Jack was tall, straight and of a splendid physique. His dark, long wavy hair, plus a becoming moustache and small goatee of the same hue, set off his pleasant face, which most of the time was tanned by his life in the open. Dark, piercing, yet kindly eyes added a distinctive touch to his pleasant countenance. He liked nice clothes and was an immaculate dresser, even when in buckskin. For his formal dress he would have only the best of cloth and that had to be fitted correctly.

A reporter for the *Rochester Evening Express* (Feb. 1, 1873), after an interview with him, wrote this descriptive paragraph:

"Texas Jack" is also a celebrated character of Western life.

Like his companion (Buffalo Bill) he is young, but has that resolute, buoyant manner, that bright, determined aspect and quick decision characteristic of men who have led lives of danger and of command. He is a little shorter than his friend, firm and strong in frame, has the same brown, healthy countenance, wears a magnificent gold cable chain, and other jewelry, which led "Buffalo Bill" to humorously describe him as the gentleman of the party.

The Earl of Dunraven, whom Jack had served as guide on at least two of his hunts in the West paid him this personal tribute:[4]

"Ah, well! . . . . it is years now since the day I first shook hands with Jack . . . and many changes have taken place since then. . . . John Omohundro, better known as Texas Jack, has gone to another and better hunting grounds. Peace be with him: he was a good and kind friend to me, a cheery companion, as brave as a lion, as gentle as a woman, always ready for anything, always willing to work, cutting down mountains of difficulties into molehills, always in a good humour, never quarreling—a better hunting companion than Jack in those days, or a more reliable friend, it would be hard to find. There was nothing mean about Jack; he was, to use one of his own western phrases, a real *white* man."

Religion to Texas Jack was a very practical thing. Even though he was of the Catholic faith, church dogmas or rituals meant very little to him. He was more concerned with the broader everyday aspects of religion—honesty in dealings with his fellow man, generous in times of need, hospitable to all, following the golden rule, assisting those less fortunate, and championing the defenseless—all were part and parcel of his philosophy of religion. And with his recognition of a supreme being, as evidenced by his church affiliation, who is there to say he was wrong in his interpretation.

The creed expressed a few days before his own death by the half-breed, Jesse Chisholm, is eminently typical of the

---

[4] "Canadian Nights," by the Earl of Dunraven. Used by permission of John Murray, Ltd., London.

everyday practice of religious principles by many of the western characters in those frontier days. He said, "I know very little about the Bible. I have no use for preachers. No man ever came to my camp hungry and went away unfed, or naked, and departed unclad. All my life I have tried to live at peace with my fellowman and be a brother to him. The rest I leave with the Great Spirit, who placed me here and whom I trust to do all things well."[5] This uneducated man who laid out the Chisholm Trail was beloved by whites and Indians alike for his honesty and fair dealings.

This old world of ours today would do well to emulate more of the homely virtues found in many of the picturesque characters of the Old West. To do so would prevent many of the heartaches of the present age in which sham and hypocrisy are so prevalent.

Small wonder that Texas Jack was held in such high regard and beloved by all who knew him, for he was a faithful exponent of the homely virtues of the Old West.

[5] John Rossel in the *Kansas State Historical Quarterly*, Feb., 1936. Used by permission.

WOOD-ENGRAVED PORTRAIT
An early portrait of Texas Jack in western attire, taken from the book "The Great Divide" by the Earl of Dunraven.

13

LEADVILLE—Trail's End

MUCH has been written concerning the fabulous City of Leadville, the town that mushroomed from a handful of crude shanties to a teeming mountain metropolis of several thousand souls, within the space of a few months' time. Little Pittsburg, New Discovery, Crysolite, Little Chief and the Matchless—nothing but names today, but in the late seventies they spelled riches untold as they poured forth ore from the deep recesses of their mine shafts. A $17 grubstake which pyramided into a cool half million dollars within a year's time set H. A. W. Tabor, a poor grocer, up as Colorado's first great Bonanza King and made him twice over a millionaire within the space of two years.

Even the most cursory description of Leadville is incomplete without the mention of Tabor, the Carbonate King. It was he who was the prime motivating figure behind the city during its first three years. Made wealthy by the ore from the hills surrounding the town, he in turn spent his money freely to promote the welfare of the new community.

Where formerly only barren rocks and sage brush dotted the terrain, buildings of logs or rough boards, and even tents, now covered the hillside as a sprawling city started its growth. Attracted to this new area of quick wealth were all types of humanity—from the most circumspect to the lowest dregs. Some came to build homes, some merely to eke out a living and a few to prey on the others. Many there were who came to prospect, hoping that they too would be among the lucky ones who would "strike it rich."

Within the space of a few month's time, temporary structures were giving way to buildings of permanence. The

young city, incorporated two short years before, was out-
growing its swaddling clothes. Churches, schools, saloons,
honky-tonks, banks, theatres and hotels were among the
additions to the rapidly growing municipality. All of this de-
velopment was not without its problems. Gambling and
crime were rampant, fights were common, and often the stac-
cato bark of six-guns could be heard above the mixed sounds
of midnight revelry and debauchery. Lawlessness seemed to
grow with the town.

All of this does not imply that Leadville was any different
from other growing frontier towns where the element of
quick wealth entered in. They were all subject to an excess
of crime and shootings. Leadville's approach to their situation
was somewhat different from that of other places. Headed
by Tabor, local guard units were formed—Leadville Guards,
Carbonate Rifles, Wolf Tone Guards, Tabor Highland
Guards and finally the Tabor Light Cavalry—the duty of
which was to patrol the streets, either day or night to preserve order, and to prevent the lawless element from gaining
an upper hand.

A description of the Tabor Light Cavalry is most interesting in that it gives a general idea as to the extent to which
the wealthy Tabor would go to do things differently—and
with much attention to himself. His light Cavalry, in red
trousers and blue coats, with shiny brass helmets, made a
flashy appearance as they rode down the street on their well-
groomed horses.[1] The Cavalry mustered fifty men, three line
and five staff officers. The officers were equipped with shiny
steel scabbards fastened to belts mounted with gold. They
wore black felt hats with a black plume and gold cord. General Tabor carried a handsome straight-edged sword engraved
on one side of the blade with the following inscriptions:
General H. A. W. Tabor C.N.A. and on the other side,
Tabor Light Cavalry.

The outfitting of the Cavalry had cost Tabor in excess of

---

[1] George F. Willison in "Here They Dug the Gold." Brentano's, New
York, 1931.

$10,000, but his liberality did not stop here. He rented a hall so that "his boys" might have a club room. The furnishings included a large oil painting of himself and one of Rev. Mackay, the company chaplain, and a photograph of the entire group. In addition, he gave the treasurer a check for $1000 for, as he expressed it, "putting the boys in good shape."

Leadville's climate at that time could not be called too severe. Yet the spectre of pneumonia, prevalent in the high, thin, mountain air and intensified by the lack of sanitary conditions, cast a sobering influence upon the young city. One day the *Daily Chronicle* was accusing the city authorities of holding midnight burials to keep the death rate from the citizens—for fear such knowledge would injure the boom. The next day the same paper would be busy trying to refute articles appearing in the newspapers throughout the country

GRAND CENTRAL THEATRE, 1880
It was in this popular theatre in Leadville that Texas Jack and his wife, Mlle. Morlacchi, made their last stage appearances.

which told of the high death rate due to the "rarefied atmosphere" of Leadville. Rather than admit the high altitude had anything to do with the prevalence of deaths by pneumonia, the *Chronicle* would counter by saying that "forty-nine cases out of fifty will be the result of bad whiskey and exposure." The fact remains, however, that in browsing through the early newspapers of Leadville one gets the distinct impression that pneumonia was the cause of the majority of deaths in those hectic days.

Leadville's leading theatre in 1879 was the Grand Central. Managed by Thomas Kemp, it was advertised as "The Largest and Best Appointed Theatre in the West."[2] This statement was to be challenged by a new show place, The Tabor Opera House, then in the process of construction. Upon this latest addition to the social life of the community Tabor lavished both money and time. It was to be more than a theatre, for the lower floor would provide for two stores. Across the second floor front of the imposing brick structure were two immense offices, both equipped with large mahogany desks. One, of course, was for Tabor himself. The other was for Bill Bush, his partner in the venture. A covered bridge joined the third floor and the Clarendon Hotel immediately to the south across St. Louis Avenue. By this means actors, actresses and celebrities could go quietly to their rooms at the hotel without going out on the street.

Entrance to the opera house proper was through two large front doors, into a spacious hall, up a flight of stairs, at the top of which to the right and left doors entered the back of the main auditorium. Another flight of stairs led to the balcony.

All Leadville awaited Thursday evening, Nov. 20, 1879, the date for the gala opening of the elegant amusement place. And, even though a sudden raid by the Vigilantes, which left two law breakers hanging from the rafters of the new city jail, cast a sobering aspect on the city, it did not for long crowd out attendance at the imposing show place.

---

[2] City Directory of Leadville, 1880.

TABOR OPERA HOUSE, 1880

Considered the finest theatre west of the Mississippi at the time it was completed in 1879 at Leadville, Colorado.

It was without doubt one of the finest theatres west of the Mississippi.[3] Seating 880 persons, the interior was beautifully frescoed; its appointments were of the first class. Furnishings included the celebrated opera chairs, with their cast iron grill work and seats and backs of red plush, manufactured by Andrew and Company of Chicago. The scenery painted by James E. Lanpher was of the most artistic, and under the mellow glow of gas light the whole interior took on a beauty that was out of this world for lovers of the legitimate stage. Even after more than seventy years, one cannot saunter through this show place of yesteryear without a feeling of nostalgia. The old dressing rooms under the stage, the spacious stage itself, the four boxes, the parquet, auditorium and finally the balcony where one may gaze down upon virtually the same interior as did those early day crowds, all conjure up visions of a past glory.

Even after the gala opening of the new opera house, the Grand Central continued to feature top dramatic talent, thus giving the Tabor the stiffest kind of competition. An advertisement of the Grand Central in the 1880 issue of the *Leadville City Directory* says, in part, "All the Leading Attractions will be Produced in Rapid Succession—DRAMAS, SPECTACULARS, and the Best Specialty Artists in the Profession."

So much for the setting of Leadville in the spring of 1880 when Texas Jack arrived upon the scene in the mining metropolis. The noted scout had come on ahead of his talented wife who was at the time finishing up an engagement at the new Adelphia Theatre in Denver. The play was *The French Spy*, a military drama. *The Rocky Mountain News* commented under the date of March 24, "M'lle Morlacchi appeared in the title role and was heartily received by her host of admirers."

It has been related that Texas Jack's purpose in going to Leadville was to see if the climate would benefit his health, which due to his spirited temperament and strenuous life had

---

[3] *The Weekly Herald* (Leadville), Nov. 15, 1879.

become somewhat impaired. This may have been true. However, there is another reason which should be taken into consideration, the lure of mining investments with their attending "get rich quick" implications. Jack loved the West and it may be that he felt this was an opportunity to get into some business enterprise and retire from the stage.

In any event there is substantiating evidence that the happy couple did not come to Leadville only for a brief theatrical stop, even though they did appear at the Grand Central. In fact Mlle. Morlacchi was featured there for many weeks in different plays, first of which was "The Black Crook" in which she had the support of her Grand Ballet Troupe.

Incidentally, this play was not without considerable interest. M. B. Leavitt in his book *Fifty Years in Theatrical Management* tells of "The Black Crook" which was first presented in New York September 12, 1866, at Niblo's Garden. He writes:

It was more than an event; it was an epoch. It was really the birth of all the ballets, burlesques, comic operas and musical comedies of the present day. It was the first time in which the feminine form divine had been displayed in all its fullness and beauty, or (in plain vernacular), it was the initial big "leg show," the first large spectacle in which womankind was made the central feature on account of the "human form divine." What a storm it raised! Pulpit and press abandoned stories and discussions about the Civil War, which had ended but little more than a year previous. The clergy were unanimous in denouncing it; the press was divided in sentiment; but the majority of the innumerable editorials that referred to it, denounced it. The public, however, rendered its own verdict by crowding the enormous auditorium of Niblo's Garden at every performance, so that (at the comparatively cheap prices obtaining in those days) the receipts averaged between $2700 and $2800 at every performance, and on several occasions even $3000.

In addition to their appearances on the stage, both Texas Jack and his wife entered into the life of the community. Jack, ever opposed to anything having to do with lawlessness, enlisted in the Tabor Light Cavalry. The experiences

STAGE SETTING OF THE TABOR OPERA HOUSE

It was in the new and beautiful Tabor Opera House that the body of Texas Jack lay in state. From its spacious stage was conducted the funeral service for this beloved scout.

of the renowned scout as a horseman and as a man of great physical strength and one to be reckoned with personally, made him a valuable addition to this newly formed group to preserve law and order.

One evening the middle part of May, Jack who had sauntered down to the station to watch the stage come in, overheard a peculiar conversation. A trio of strangers more than slightly "in their cups" permitted words to escape that gave away a plan which, had they been sober they would not have revealed so close to the ears of Texas Jack.

They had learned that a man of wealth was in town to look after some of his extensive holdings. Reasoning among themselves that he would have considerable cash on his person, they planned to make sure of his departure on the next day's stage. Taking a short cut to a particular hazardous spot where the stage coach would have to slow down, they would proceed to "relieve" the capitalist of his "ready means."

Overhearing their plans Jack sought the assistance of a couple of friends. They too took a little trip, but not with the same purpose in mind. Reaching the spot mentioned by the robbers, they hid their horses a short distance away and proceeded to take cover out of sight behind some large rocks to await the three robbers—and the stage coach.

Before long the gangsters arrived and hid themselves among the rocks below the positions taken by Jack and his friends. Hardly had the late arrivals taken their place until the rumbling of the wheels over loose rocks told of the approach of the coach. Just as the six-in-hand, driven by the veteran driver Jake Timberlake, rounded the sharp turn, the startling "Hands Up" command of the robbers rang out. Amidst the screeching of the brakes, the coach rolled to a stop as startled and frightened passengers peered out the window in apprehension.

Scarcely had the stage stopped, however, when another deep and commanding voice broke the stillness. This time it was Texas Jack who was speaking and his voice was directed at the three robbers who had suddenly found themselves gazing into the buisness end of the revolvers of Jack and his two companions.

It was but a matter of minutes until a relieved stage-driver, and passengers, had the three bandits securely tied and placed on top of the coach to be taken to the nearest stop to await the "demands of justice."

Refusing offers of money for their part in thwarting the robbers, Jack and his friends returned to Leadville happy in the thought of a job well done.

During these weeks the enterprising Morlacchi had opened up a dancing studio for the kiddies. Under the heading, MORLACCHI TEACHING THE 15 PUZZLE, *The Daily Democrat* (April 21, 1880) had this unusual paragraph:

It is amusing to witness the patience exhibited by Mlle. Morlacchi in her endeavors to imbue her youthful pupils with the idea of 15, 14, 13 positions, and only two block-heads—no legs—to put in them. She is teaching one little tot to dance who isn't knee-high to a Republican majority.

Fate was to prove unkind to the young couple so desirous of settling in Leadville for a while. Late in May the famous scout contracted a heavy cold, a thing to which at first he paid but scant attention. After all, what was a mere cold to one who had endured all sorts of exposures and was accustomed to the vicissitudes of frontier life. It was only upon the insistent urgings of his devoted wife and of his friend Major T. C. Howard, at whose home they were living at the time, that he finally consented to take to his bed, firmly convinced that in a day or so he would be back to normal. Such was not to be, for in the delay the cold had turned into pneumonia and that into quick consumption. In spite of all the skilled physicians, headed by Dr. Henry Cook, could do, Texas Jack did not respond, but lapsed into unconsciousness. At 7:30 on Monday morning June 28, 1880, the beloved plainsman, scout, Indian fighter, guide and actor closed his eyes in the sleep from which none ever awakens.

Immediately upon learning of the death of Texas Jack, Edwin F. Knowles, manager of the new Tabor Opera House, extended his sympathy and offered the use of the beautiful auditorium for the funeral. The offer was accepted by the bereaved wife and friends, and there amidst the setting of the beautiful theatre, and in the West he loved, was conducted the final services for John B. "Texas Jack" Omohundro.

In the absence of Father Henry Robinson, who was out of the city due to illness, the services were conducted by the Rev. Thomas J. Mackay, Episcopal Chaplain of the Tabor Light Cavalry. A choir composed of members of Fay Templeton's opera company, which was playing in Leadville at the time, furnished music for the occasion. Following the obsequies at the Opera House, which was attended by all who could crowd into the spacious show place, the funeral cortege took its leave. Led by a fifty-piece brass band, followed by Jack's former comrades of the Tabor Light Cavalry under the leadership of the Hon. H. A. W. Tabor, then Lieut. Gov. of Colorado, and Rev. Mackay, the procession moved up Harrison Avenue to Eighth Street and thence westward to the newly plotted cemetery.[4] At the graveside, Mr. Tabor made a few closing remarks complimentary to his friend Texas Jack.[5] The service was concluded by the firing of a military salute and the sounding of taps, a tribute to J. B. Omohundro, soldier of the Confederacy.

There in the quiet solitude of Evergreen Cemetery the great scout sleeps the last sleep. The wind plays an everlasting requiem as it blows softly through the stately pines. Nearby in all its majestic beauty stands the eternal snow-capped Mount Massive as though it were a sentinel on guard to assure that he will rest in peace until the end of time.

Both newspapers carried stories of the passing of the gallant scout. The following paragraphs are taken from *The Daily Chronicle* under the date of June 28, 1880:

DEMISE OF TEXAS JACK, the Noted Scout and Actor
Death of "Texas Jack"

John Baker Omohundro, better known under the sobriquet

---

[4] Evergreen Cemetery was plotted and laid out in November of 1879. Maj. Jesse L. Pritchard was Superintendent of the work. (*Leadville Herald*, Nov. 8, 1879.)
[5] David Karsner in "*Silver Dollar.*"

"Texas Jack," died at the residence of Major Howard, on Fourth Street, at 7:30 o'clock this morning. The primary cause of death was pneumonia contracted from exposure, which commenced a month since, but last week it developed into rapid consumption. Dr. Cook was called in attendance day before yesterday and succeeded in rallying the patient to such a degree that his friends deemed a temporary cure would be effected, but at three o'clock this morning a sudden change occurred and he sank rapidly, unconscious to the last.

He was noted as a cool, intrepid Indian fighter, government scout and ranchman, but was never a desperado or even a quarrelsome man, and it is believed had no white man's blood upon his hands, unless drawn in legitimate warfare. In fact, his most intimate acquaintances refer to his kindly disposition and his exceptional muscular strength.

Soon after the commencement of the war, he enlisted in the Confederate Cavalry . . . Like all who have figured in this capacity, his experience contained much of interest, but he was very reticent and would seldom be induced to talk about himself or any incident of which he was known to be a chief participant, but much has been told to his advantage by comrades who were with him on various occasions.

At the close of the war he resumed his career on the plains, and became again prominent as a U. S. Government scout, and was thrown into association with W. F. Cody (Buffalo Bill) and J. B. Hickok (Wild Bill). He also acted as frontier correspondent for the *New York Herald*.

When Ned Buntline wrote the famous novelette, entitled "Buffalo Bill," it caused such a sensation that over 350,000 copies were sold throughout the United States. Fred G. Maeder, a well known actor and dramatist, conceived the idea of placing it before the people in the shape of a play depicting the prevalent eastern idea of life on the border. It was produced as such at the Bowery Theatre, and Cody, who was at the time in that city, witnessed it from a private box. A proposition was made him to appear in the principal character himself, and after much deliberation he consented. More means were required than the managers at that time possessed, and Cody bethought himself of his old comrade, Omohundro, who had been quite prosperous in some late ventures.

So the twain were united in the enterprise, and the successful career of Buffalo Bill and Texas Jack is well known, and their highly colored portraits as exhibited on the walls have made their faces familiar to every schoolboy in the land.

Flushed with success, they succeeded, after one year's suppli-
cation, in inducing Wild Bill to join them, but he did not remain
long as he did not feel comfortable in the hotels and convention-
alities of the East, and speedily returned to his frontier life, and
this hero of many a hard fought hand to hand encounter soon
after met his death at the hands of a dastardly assassin, who shot
him from behind his back while sitting at a gambling table in
Deadwood, Dakota. During the summer interims, when not acting, both Cody and Omohundro occupied their time in the West,
either as scouts or ranchmen, and Texas Jack acted as guide for
several parties of titled Englishmen, who were anxious to participate in life on the plains.

He was married to Mlle. Morlacchi, the famous danseuse, who
was at the time the leading star in her profession, and at the zenith
of artistic and financial prosperity. It was a genuine case of true
love, and the couple have never had a quarrel in all these years.
Madame Morlacchi is one of those ladies whose exemplary conduct and genial disposition under all circumstances, have caused
her name to be a synonym for all that is good and praiseworthy
in her profession. She has been obliged to resign her situation at
the theater in order to give her sole attention to her husband,
and for the past four days she has been almost without nourish-
ment or sleep. While sitting gazing at his corpse about half an
hour after his demise, her face set in solid despair, her whole
frame fixed in that absorbent grief which gives no outward
demonstration, she fell to the floor an inanimate mass. It is
feared by her friends that exhaustion and nervous prostration
have already placed her life in jeopardy.

Texas Jack was a member of the Tabor Light Cavalry, under
its former organization, and the members are notified elsewhere
to attend his funeral, which will take place from the Tabor Opera
House, which has been gratuitously tendered by Manager
Knowles for that purpose. In recognition of his brave deeds, he
will receive a soldier's funeral, and martial salute will be fired
over his grave.

The entire dramatic and varied profession, as well as all
friends and acquaintances, are invited to join in the obsequies
tomorrow afternoon.

The Daily Democrat in its issue of June 29, 1880, carried
this brief paragraph:

DEATH OF "TEXAS JACK"

John Baker Omohundro, popularly known as "Texas Jack,"
departed this life at the residence of Major Howard yesterday

morning at an early hour. In the death of Texas Jack there ends the life of a man whose career has been filled with the most wonderful vicissitudes, and the last of a man who at all times was surrounded by a host of genial, warm and staunch companions. His wife, M'lle Morlacchi, is inconsolable, and is at present unconscious. The funeral will take place this afternoon at two o'clock. M'lle Morlacchi has the sympathy of the entire city in this the great sorrow of her life. The body will lie in state at the opera house and will be interred with military honors.

It will be noted that both accounts gave his middle name as Baker. This does not agree with his birth record in which Burwell is given as the name. It is very possible that later in life he adopted the name in honor of his own mother whose maiden name was Baker. Such individual prerogatives are not uncommon and it may have been his way of paying tribute to the memory of his mother.

Following the death of her distinguished husband, Mlle. Morlacchi took leave of her troupe and left for her home in Lowell, Mass. There is no record of her having returned to the stage. She lived quietly with her sister in their two residences in Lowell and East Billerica and endeared herself to the two communities by her many acts of kindness.[6]

On August 18, 1885, sorrow again came into the life of Mlle. Morlacchi. This time in was caused by the death of her sister Angelina with whom she shared her home. Even at this time the beloved danseuse of the stage was the victim of an incurable disease which was to claim her own life a few short months hence.

These brief lines from a lengthy article in the July 24, 1886, issue of *The Lowell Daily Citizen* furnish the details of her passing:

A NOTED DANSEUSE GONE

Mrs. Josephine Omohundro, widow of J. B. Omohundro, better known as Texas Jack died at her summer residence in East Billerica, Friday, aged 39 years and 9 months . . . The sisters were highly esteemed by their neighbors for their many kind acts . . . The sister, Angelina Morlacchi, died about a year ago.

---

[6] *Lowell Daily Citizen*, July 24, 1886.

For the last nine months the deceased has suffered severely from cancer, which eventually caused her death yesterday at eleven o'clock at her Billerica home. The funeral will occur from St. Joseph's Church in this city Monday morning at nine o'clock when a Solemn High Mass will be celebrated.

Other accounts report that the entire town turned out. In the church where the services were held were the Methodists, Baptists and Catholic clergymen. Some of the stores were closed. All denominations mourned her. The community mourned her memory. This was a beautiful tribute to the petite ballet dancer whom the community had grown to love as one of its own.

In the crowd of mourners there was one who, in spite of his dignified bearing and his long flowing hair and side burns, all but escaped notice. It was the one to whom Mlle. Morlacchi was ever the goddess and the one the gallant scout, Texas Jack, had beaten for the hand of the lovely lady— Major John M. Burke. It was he who had been her and her husband's manager in the days past. Saddened beyond words, he took his leave after the services to again take up his work with the man who was to be his idol for the remaining thirty-nine years of his life—W. F. "Buffalo Bill" Cody.

Critics may argue pro and con about the ability and stature of this or that western character, but a close scrutiny of contemporary accounts and the comments of those who knew him intimately bears out the statement that Texas Jack was beloved by all. Whatever faults he may have had, his loyalty, honesty, faithfulness and devotion to duty were the traits for which he would be remembered by his host of friends. These, plus his modesty, ability and integrity have assured for him a permanent place among the truly great of the Old West.

The following poem written at the time of Jack's death[7] by his old friend, Major Sam S. Hall (Buckskin Sam) of the

---

[7] *Beadle's Boy's Library of Sport, Story and Adventure* (large size) Vol. I, No. 17 (April 5, 1882).
Beadle's Boys Library (small size) Vol. III, No. 27 entitled "Buckskin Sam's Wild Ride" by Col. Prentiss Ingraham.

Texas Rangers, is eloquent testimony of the esteem in which
the scout was held by his "pards."

BUCKSKIN SAM'S TRIBUTE TO TEXAS JACK

No more will he turn the wild stampede
With whoop and yell on galloping steed;
No more take the red-man's moccasined track,
'Mid bow-string's twang and rifle's crack;
No more with rare skill his lasso whirl,
Or through the air his dread bowie hurl;
No more be poised on the mustang's back,
And drive wild herds on the northern track;
No more the "black snake" deftly swing;
No more on the Llanos will his rifle ring—
The far-away trails his feet have trod
Will know him no more—he has gone to God!

Lay him to rest in his narrow home
Beneath the sky, earth's natural dome,
Where Southern verdure luxuriant grows,
Ne'er withered by icy Northern snows;
There, 'neath the Spanish moss and pine,
Where myriads of flowering creepers twine,
Let him repose in Nature's wild,
Fit resting place for Nature's child.

There would I dig in grassy bank,
Afar from noisy cow-bells clank,
Where oft the red-man leaves his track,
A fitting grave for Texas Jack.
There would I lay him down to rest
Amid the scenes that he loved best;
I'd dig his lone grave long and wide,
And lay his rifle by his side;
I'd coil his lariat 'round his feet,
His serape use for a winding sheet.
But be his grave in wildwood made
Or in the city's busy mart,
Carve on the stone, in words of gold,
"HERE LIES A NOBLE HEART."

14

A FINAL TRIBUTE

EVEN to the last, Mlle. Morlacchi's thoughts were of her noble husband. In her will dated May 19, 1886, a few short weeks before her death she included this significant provision:[1]

Five hundred dollars to be expended by my Executor hereinafter named in procuring a suitable monument for the grave of my husband, John B. Omohundro at Leadville, Colorado.

It is most unfortunate that this last request was never carried out by her friend, Henry A. McGlenen of Boston, who was appointed executor. Other provisions of the will were followed; why this desire of the dying wife to honor her husband was not fulfilled, will in all probability always remain a mystery.

For many long years the grave of Texas Jack had a unique tombstone—erected and cared for by the hands of his Leadville friends who cherished his noble manhood. A western newspaper under date of August 10, 1887 carried a sketch of the stone together with a brief article under a Leadville date line entitled, "Texas Jack's Grave." The story in part:

While Buffalo Bill is raising such a furor in England, and while the Britishers, from the royal Prince down to the meanest costermonger, are doing the Wild West Show with vigor, there are a few here who recall that other great cowboy of the footlights as well as the foothills, and many a visit has been paid to one quaintly marked grave in the gravelly burying ground of this far-up city. The grave is that of Texas Jack.
He had many points in common with his fellow-showman from the plains. They both were known the country over by their cowboy nicknames, and they were the twin deities to the small boy with an Indian-killing weakness. In some respects the Hon.

---

[1] Registry of Probate, Billerica, Mass.

J. B. Omohundro was a better stage subject than the Hon. William Cody. He could orate, and filled out a border drama in fine style. He came East, and met Morlacchi, the famous dancer. It was a love match between the rough-and-ready dashing buckrider and the Italian woman trained in the school of La Scala. She little dreamed that she was to meet her fate when she came as the queen of the ballet to fill engagements in this country. The two loved—the gallant border swain and the warm-blooded dark-eyed Italian sylph. They married and could not enjoy each other's society enough. It was while filling an engagement in this pneumonia city that Texas Jack went the way of a majority of the 3,300 who lie about him, and he succumbed to the dread lung trouble.

TEXAS JACK'S TOMBSTONE.

His grave slab would have suited his ideas to a dot. There is the cartridge belt, the bowie-knife and guns; below, his Winchester. Then a portrait of his pony, Yellow Chief, duly labelled, and finally a few words of the famous man who rests so quietly below:

Sacred to the Memory
of
Texas Jack
(J. B. Omohundro)
Died June 28, 1880
39, Pneumonia

Morlacchi respected his memory greatly, and showed her feelings by making a permanent retirement from the stage. Alive, Buffalo Bill is giving England a genuine sensation. Dead, his associate, Texas Jack, finds a grave in one of the historic cemeteries of the country, far skyward in the rich soil of his favorite Colorado.

Even though the marker at the grave of Texas Jack gives his age as 39, he was in reality but 33 years of age at the time of his unfortunate death.

On Monday August 31, 1908, Leadville had an interesting visitor. Let the *Herald Democrat* tell of it in its issue of September 1st:

Memories of frontier days on mountain and plain were recalled yesterday by a visit to Leadville of Major John M. Burke, intimate friend of Col. William F. Cody (Buffalo Bill) and his personal representative in advance of the Wild West exhibition which appears here next Saturday.

Major Burke himself was a plainsman and scout, and was closely connected with all the characters of early western life. Since 1881 he has been associated with Buffalo Bill in his instructive exhibition of an interesting and important period in the country's progress to which has recently been added a congress of rough riders of the world.

The Major was a frequent visitor to Leadville in the early day of this city, and had as his special friend here, John Omohundro, better known as "Texas Jack." Yesterday morning he drove to Evergreen Cemetery where Jack lies buried, and placed a wreath of flowers upon his grave . . .

His long association with Buffalo Bill, Wild Bill and Texas Jack caused Major Burke to grow reminiscent of the three and aroused a feeling of regret over the death of such a promising young career as Texas Jack. The Major treasures among his most valued possessions, a picture of the three noted scouts taken together at Syracuse, N. Y. while they were visiting in the east in 1874.

On "Circus Day," Saturday, September 5, 1908, the same newspaper printed this significant observation:

While here today Col. Cody will drive to Evergreen Cemetery where his old friend and comrade, Texas Jack, lies buried. He will place a bouquet of flowers on the grave, and it is probable that the sight of the simple cross which now marks "Jack's" last resting place will prompt him to start some action with reference to the much discussed movement of substituting a monument more substantial and worthy of one of the bravest frontiersmen of the plains."

In its Sunday, Sept. 6, 1908, issue *The Herald Democrat* carried the following descriptive review of the renowned Buffalo Bill's visit to the grave of his old pard of the plains:

CODY HONORS
TEXAS JACK

No tribute more beautiful than that paid by Col. William F. Cody, "Buffalo Bill," to his old friend and comrade, John B. Omohundro, "Texas Jack," just as the glorious western sun slowly sinking behind majestic Mount Massive, cast its mellow shadows through the pines of Evergreen Cemetery yesterday evening, was ever rendered by a living man to one who has gone before.

If the spirit of "Texas Jack" were able to hover over the little mound that contains his mortal remains he would have been gratified by the ceremonies in honor of his memory. They were the kind of ceremonies that his plain, rough, honest character would have asked could he have chosen—brief, simple and unaffected, but oh, how impressive!

Col. Cody himself was the principal speaker; the Rev. Alexander Pringle of this city, offered prayer; the Wild West band played appropriate musical selections; Prof. John M. Kerns, who led the band at the funeral of the deceased, stood close by; around the grave were gathered hundreds of Leadville citizens and rough riders, soldiers, cowboys, Indians and other attachés of the exhibition.

Before leaving the cemetery, Col. Cody arranged with Manager William Youe of the Leadville Monument Works, for the erection of a substantial stone over the grave, in place of the humble wooden slab that now marks the last resting place of the scout and pioneer Leadvilleite.

The scene at the grave was most impressive.

It is probable that in the history of all this country, of the entire world; a sight more unique has never been witnessed in a cemetery.

Gathered around the resting place of the Confederate scout, cowboy, plainsman and Indian fighter were grouped representatives of nearly every nation of the globe. To add to the picturesqueness of the occasion, all were garbed in their native

PARADE IN LEADVILLE

This parade up Harrison Street is believed to include units of the
noted Tabor Light Cavalry . . . an organization of which Texas Jack
was a member.

CODY HONORS TEXAS JACK

Veteran Scout With Indians and Cowboys at Grave of Famous Fighter.

ORDERS MONUMENT ERECTED

No tribute more beautiful than that paid by Col. William F. Cody, "Buffalo Bill," to his old friend and comrade, John B. Omohundro, "Texas Jack," just as the glorious western sun slowly sinking behind majestic Mount Massive, cast its mellow shadows through the pines of Evergreen cemetery yesterday evening, was ever rendered by a living man to one who has gone before.

If the spirit of "Texas Jack" were able to hover over the little mound that contains his mortal remains he would have been gratified by the ceremonies in honor of his memory. They were the kind of ceremonies that his plain, rough, honest character would have asked could he have chosen—brief, simple and unaffected, but

CODY HONORS TEXAS JACK, 1908

From a front page story in *The Herald Democrat*, Leadville, Colorado, Sunday, Sept. 6, 1908 describing in detail the visit of Buffalo Bill and his Circus troupe to the grave of Texas Jack.

costumes, their garments appearing in strange contrast with the solemnity of the occasion.

In the rear of the semi-circle stood a dozen cavalrymen, late of the United States Army, against whose predecessors Jack waged a persistent warfare as one of Col. "Jeb" Stuart's most faithful scouts.

With this soldiery, representatives of several Indian tribes—the Sioux and the Utes—stood silently by in war paint and feathers. Memories of the bitterness with which the plainsman had fought their forefathers for possession of the very ground upon which they stood, gave way to feelings of admiration and respect for his bravery and sturdy frontier life.

Gathered near the front of the picture was a crowd of Mexican vaqueros, whose ancestors were a natural enemy of the man whose memory they gathered to honor, during the time he served as a cowboy on the Texas plains.

At their side, and across the grave, facing them, stood a band of Russian Cossacks. Next to the daring riders of the great northern empire, a group of brown skinned, square shouldered Japanese warriors looked on with solemn faces, the representatives of the two countries who so recently engaged in bitter warfare.

Each separate group attired in its distinguished dress, representatives of the British cavalry, Arabian patrol and German horseman added to the variety of colors and nationalities.

Impressed by the ceremony second only to Col. Cody himself was the crowd of cowboys, whose experiences on the plains have been similar to those of the dead friend of their present day chieftain. These men felt that the old scout was one of them. To them the service was of greater import than to those whose life has been spent in some other pursuit. Tears welled to the eyes of many of these strong-muscled, large-hearted men. It was one of their comrades whom they were honoring—a man whom they knew and whose life was their life, though they had never seen him.

At the outer edge, civilians from everyday life added a bit of metropolitanism to the scene.

After the band had discoursed a few numbers, Col. Cody with head uncovered, his silvery locks tossed light by the evening breeze, addressed the strange crowd briefly. He spoke as follows:

"My friends, perhaps many of you do not know this man whom we have gathered to honor. No doubt you would like to know something of him, who was one of my dearest and most intimate friends.

GRANITE MARKER AT THE GRAVE OF
TEXAS JACK

A simple, yet attractive granite monument marks the
resting place of this noted scout of the Old West. It was
placed there in grateful memory by his old friends, Col.
Wm. F. Cody ("Buffalo Bill"), Maj. John M. Burke
("Arizona John") and a devoted admirer, Johnny Baker,
foster son of Buffalo Bill.

"John B. Omohundro, better known as 'Texas Jack,' was a
Virginian by birth. The blood of the Powhatan Indians flowed
in his veins. He was of proud and noble birth.

"During the Civil War he was a member of the cavalry command under Col. 'Jeb' Stuart of the Confederate Army. He was
one of his most trusted and faithful scouts and performed almost
invaluable service for him.

"After the war he drifted westward and located in Texas, where he took up the hazardous work of a cowboy. He was one of the original Texas cowboys, when life on the plains was a hardship and a trying duty.

"When they began to drive the cattle to the northern country, he engaged in that occupation, following the herds northward, and returning after each trip for another herd.

"Finally he located at North Platte, Nebraska. It was there that I first met him. He was an expert trailer and scout. I soon recognized this and tried to secure his appointment in United States service. But the authorities were unwilling to hire discharged Confederate scouts, so I had to take the matter to the secretary of war. After much persuasion I was given permission to hire him.

"In this capacity I learned to know him and to respect his bravery and ability. He was a whole-souled, brave, generous, good-hearted man.

"Later he and I went East to go into the show business. He was the first to do a lasso act upon the stage.

"After a short career with the show we again went West. That was in 1873 . . . We returned East and again went on the stage. It was during this tour of the large cities that he met and married M'lle Morlacchi, a famous dancer, who traveled with him.

"After I left him, he and she continued to travel. They came to Leadville, where she was engaged as a performer. Becoming attached to the place, my friend and his wife remained for a while.

"It was while here that he was stricken with pneumonia, which was then prevalent. He succumbed, and was buried here under this mound by his many friends.

"Among those who contributed to the ceremony at that time was Mr. Kerns, who is here now, and who remembers the manly traits of poor Jack.

"Jack was an old friend of mine and a good one.

"Instead of this board which now marks his grave, we will soon have erected a more substantial monument, one more worthy of a brave and good man.

"May he rest in peace."

At the conclusion of Col. Cody's remarks, Rev. Pringle offered prayer as follows:

"O Thou God of nations, Thou ruler of kings and princes, Lord over all, blessed forever more; we bless Thy holy name

'BUFFALO BILL' AT
GRAVE OF HIS OLD
FRIEND 'TEXAS JACK'

Reproduced from an unknown newspaper, this photograph shows the renowned Buffalo Bill at the grave of his old pard Texas Jack.

for this goodly land we call our own, this land of mountain and valley, of plain and prairie, of fruitful field and garden, where peace and plenty crown the days and the years.

"We thank Thee for the good work of all who have gone before us, the fruit of whose labors we now enjoy, for the hardy pioneer who braved the perils of the frontier, who tamed the wilderness, and built for us and for God. We thank Thee for those who were the advance guards of civilization, who gallantly faced brave enemies, and by whose courage lovely vales and sunny slopes were made safe for the husbandman, his wife and little ones. We bless Thy name for those who have finished their warfare and now rest from their labors. And do Thou grant that when our last hour cometh we may be neither troubled nor dismayed, but trusting in Thy goodness and mercy, we may fall peacefully asleep and obtain a happy entrance unto Thine everlasting habitations.

"We ask Thy blessing to rest on this service of love in memory of a departed comrade who was fearless in combat and loyal in friendship. May each one of us be as true and courageous in our several places as he was in his. His mistakes be Thou pleased to forgive; his shortcomings blot out and remember no more, for Thy mercy's sake which is so great.

"And grant, O Thou Father of us all, that on this heaven-blest land Thy children of every faith and of so many races may live and work in peace, in quietness, and fraternal love, inspired by reverence for our common Lord, and by lofty devotion to our common country.

"And now may the Lord bless and keep you. The Lord make his face shine upon you and be gracious unto you. The Lord lift up His countenance upon you and give you peace. Amen."

The band played "Nearer My God to Thee," and the assemblage dispersed with a better feeling for the world and what it contains and with added respect and admiration for Col. Cody, whose true manliness and whole-heartedness was never better shown.

The world famous Buffalo Bill had not forgotten his old friend and comrade of the plains and stage, Texas Jack.

* * *

Sleep On Texas Jack in your silent grave until Gabriel blows his horn . . . and the old scouts gather for that last roundup in the skies.

TEXAS JACK

He hailed from the Lone Star state
    Down in the great southwest.
He scouted and ran into
    Many a hostile Indian nest.

He quelled the cattle rustlers
    Across the burning sand.
He stopped the raids of greasers
    When he crossed the Rio Grande.

He later acted on the stage
    And showed the old time west.
He has a place in history
    With the winning of the west.

He was a scout and plainsman,
    A hunter and a guide.
He has gone to join his partners
    Who are on the other side.

                     —Col. Charles D. Randolph
                      "Buckskin Bill"

TEXAS JACK—A Chronology

1846   July 26. Born at "Pleasure Hill" near Palmyra, Fluvanna County, Virginia. Fourth child of J. B. Omohundro and Catherine S. Baker Omohundro.

1861   Worked on the cattle ranches in Texas where he received the training which proved so useful in later life.

1863   Served as a headquarters courier under Gen. J. B. Floyd, C. S. A.

1864   Feb. 15. Enlisted as a private in Co. G, 5th Regiment, Virginia Cavalry, Confederate States Army from Fluvanna County, Virginia.

       May 11. Reported to have been the scout who delivered a dispatch to Gen. J. E. B. Stuart a few minutes before the General was shot.

       June 20. Admitted to Confederate States General Hospital at Charlottesville, Virginia.

       Nov. 16. His mother died after a lingering illness.

1865   The boat upon which he had embarked at New Orleans, and which was bound for Texas, encountered a severe storm and was finally forced to land on the West coast of Florida. Here he hunted deer and taught school for some months.

1867-1868   Drove cattle over the old Chisholm Trail into Kansas and Nebraska.

       Rescued and befriended a small lad whose parents had been killed by the Indians. When the boy grew to young manhood he took the name of Texas Jack in appreciation of his benefactor.

1869   Aug. Spent part of the summer around Fort Hays (Kansas) where he made the acquaintance of and formed a friendship with California Joe and Wild Bill Hickok.

       In the employ of a Mr. Brown he drove a herd of longhorn Texas cattle to the vicinity of North Platte, Nebraska.

1870-1871   Buffalo hunter, guide and scout in western Nebraska. His hunting companion of these years was Doc W. F. Carver, later to become the world's champion rifle shot.

1872   Lived at Cottonwood Springs which was on the Fort
McPherson military post.

Jan. Assisted Buffalo Bill Cody as a guide on the Royal
Buffalo Hunt for the Grand Duke Alexis of Russia.

April-May. Employed by the U. S. as a scout under the
command of Col. J. J. Reynolds, 3rd U. S. Cavalry.
Served as a guide for Co. B in the pursuit of a band of
marauding Indians.

June. Assisted Charles McDonald and his son W. H.
brand cattle at Cottonwood Springs.

Aug.-Sept.-Oct. Deputy U. S. Agent under Maj. Troth
(Indian Agent for Nebraska). In this connection he served
as Trail Agent for the Pawnees, on their summer hunt,
by the direction of Generals Sheridan and Ord.

Oct.-Nov. Served as a guide for the Earl of Dunraven
and party.

Dec. 16. Appeared on the stage with Buffalo Bill and
Ned Buntline in the premiere showing of the *Scouts of
the Prairie.*

Met and became an admirer of Mlle. Josephine Morlacchi the noted danseuse, and a member of the cast.

1873   Toured with the *Scouts of the Prairie* in company with
Buffalo Bill, Ned Buntline and Mlle. Morlacchi until the
season ended at Port Jervis on June 16th.

May. Entertained members of his family in Richmond
during the several days the show was playing there.

July-Aug. Hunted with Buffalo Bill in western Nebraska.
Also acted as guide for a Mr. Scott (a Chicago hatter),
Eugene Overton and Elisha Green (Remington's son-in-
law).

Aug. 31. Married Mlle. Josephine Morlacchi at Rochester,
N. Y.

Sept. Started his second season on the stage. The play
was *Scouts of the Plains.* Wild Bill Hickok replaced
Buntline for the second season.

He and his wife purchased Suffolk Hall in Lowell, Mass.
This became their permanent home when not on the road
with their shows.

1874   Starred in *Scouts of the Plains* until the season closed late
in the spring.

March. Wild Bill Hickok left the show at Rochester, N. Y.

Fall and Winter. Served as guide for the Earl of Dunraven and his party on their hunt in the Yellowstone
country.

His old friend Doc Carver was also with the party for part of the time.

1875-1876 Continued his stage career with Buffalo Bill for the 1875-76 season.

1876 Aug. Scouted and wrote for the *New York Herald*. While in company with Captains Frederick Benteen and MacDougal of the Seventh Cavalry he met Lt. Hugh L. Scott (later Maj. Gen.) in St. Paul. At the time he was on his way east to join his wife in Philadelphia.

Fall. Served as guide for Sir John Reid and his cousin, Mr. Eaton, both of England.

1877 Feb. Interviewed by a writer for *Spirit of the Times*.

March. Wrote for *Spirit of the Times*, a New York publication. Articles in the March 3, 17 and 24th issues.

April. As he was being interviewed by a reporter of *Spirit of the Times* their staff artist made a graphic sketch of him in his picturesque western attire.

May. He and his own combination played at the De Bar's Opera House in St. Louis.

1878 Feb. Appeared with his own troupe at the Olympic Theatre in New York, the show, *Scouts of the Plains*.

1880 March 16. Played in the new Adelphia Theatre in Denver, the show, *The Trapper's Daughter*.

March 25. Appeared at a Chestnut Street Theatre in Leadville.

May. Volunteered as a member of the Tabor Light Cavalry of Leadville.

June 28. Died of pneumonia at the home of Major Howard.

* * * *

1886 July 23. Death of his widow, Mlle. Morlacchi, at Lowell, Mass.

1908 Sept. 5. In a visit to the grave of Texas Jack with his entire Wild West Circus troupe, Buffalo Bill paid tribute to his old "pard" of the Plains, and ordered a beautiful granite marker placed at his grave.

BIBLIOGRAPHY
Books

BLISS, FRANK E., *The Life of Hon. William F. Cody known as Buffalo Bill.* Hartford, Conn., 1879.

BRUCE, ROBERT, *The Fighting Norths and Pawnee Scouts.* New York, Brooklyn Eagle Press, 1932.

BUEL, J. W., *Heroes of the Plains.* San Francisco, A. L. Bancroft & Co., 1881.

BURKE, JOHN M., *Buffalo Bill, from Prairie to Palace.* Chicago, Rand, McNally & Co., 1893.

CATTERMOLE, E. G., *Famous Frontiersmen, Pioneers and Scouts.* New York, M. A. Donohue & Co.

CHAPMAN, ARTHUR, *The Pony Express.* New York, G. P. Putnam's Sons, 1932.

CODY, LOUISA FREDERICI, *Memories of Buffalo Bill.* New York, D. Appleton & Co., 1920.

CODY, WILLIAM F., *The Adventures of Buffalo Bill.* New York, Harper & Brothers, 1904.

CODY, COL. W. F., *Autobiography of Buffalo Bill, Story of the Wild West.*

CODY, COL. W. F., *Buffalo Bill's Life Story, an Autobiography.* New York, Cosmopolitan Book Corporation, 1920.

CODY, WILLIAM F., *Story of the Wild West and Campfire Chats.* Chicago, Charles C. Thompson Co., 1888.

CODY, WILLIAM F., *Life and Adventures of Buffalo Bill.* New York, Willey Book Company, 1927.

CONNELLEY, W. E., *Wild Bill and His Era.* New York, Press of the Pioneers, 1933.

COX, JAMES, *Historical and Biographical Record of the Cattle Industry, and the Cattlemen of Texas.* St. Louis, 1895.

CUSTER, GEN. GEORGE A., *Wild Life on the Plains and Horrors of Indian Warfare.*

DAY, DONALD, *The Autobiography of Will Rogers.* Boston, Houghton, Mifflin Company, 1949.

DUNRAVEN, EARL OF, *Canadian Nights.* London, Smith, Elder & Co., 1914.

DUNRAVEN, EARL OF, *The Great Divide.* London, Chatto and Windus, 1876.

DUNRAVEN, EARL OF, *Hunting in the Yellowstone*. New York, Macmillian and Co., 1925.

FREEMAN, DOUGLAS SOUTHALL, *Lee's Lieutenants*. New York, Charles Scribners & Sons, 1944.

GARST, SHANNON, *Buffalo Bill*. New York, Pocket Book, Jrs., 1950.

GRISWOLD, DON & JEAN, *The Carbonate Camp Called Leadville*. Denver, University of Denver Press, 1952.

HADLEY, JAMES A., *A Royal Buffalo Hunt*. Topeka, Kansas, Kansas State Historical Society, 1908.

HARRIS, JOEL CHANDLER, *On the Wings of Occasion*.

HEIZMANN, ASST. SURGEON CHARLES L., *A Report on the Hygiene of the U. S. Army*. Washington, 1875.

HYDE, GEORGE E., *Pawnee Indians*. Denver, University of Denver Press, 1951.

JOHANNSEN, ALBERT, *The House of Beadle and Adams and Its Dime and Nickel Novels*. Norman, Okla., University of Oklahoma Press, 1950.

KARSNER, DAVID, *Silver Dollar*.

KINGSLEY, DR. CHARLES H., *Notes on Sport and Travel*. London, Macmillian and Co., 1900.

LEAVITT, M. B., *Fifty Years in Theatrical Management*. New York, Broadway Publishing Co., 1912.

MAURY, GEN. DABNEY H., *Recollections of a Virginian*. New York, Charles Scribner's Sons, 1894.

MILNER & FORREST, JOE E. & EARLE R., *California Joe*. Caldwell, Idaho, The Caxton Printers, Ltd., 1935.

MONAGHAN, JAY, *The Great Rascal*. New York, Little, Brown & Co., 1952.

OMOHUNDRO, MALVERN H., *The Omohundro Genealogical Record*. Staunton, Virginia, McClure Printing Company, 1951.

OTERO, MIGUEL A., *My Life on the Frontier*. New York, Press of the Pioneers, 1935-39.

POND, FRED E., *Life and Adventures of Ned Buntline*. New York, The Cadmus Book Shop, 1919.

ROOT & CONNELLEY, FRANK A. & W. E., *The Overland Stage to California*.

SCOTT, MAJ. GEN. HUGH L., *Some Memories of a Soldier*. New York, The Century Company, 1928.

THOMASON, JOHN W., JR., *JEB Stuart*. New York, Chas. Scribner's Sons, 1930.

WALSH, RICHARD J., *The Making of Buffalo Bill*. Indianapolis, Bobbs-Merrill Company, 1928.

WARE, EUGENE F., *The Indian War of 1864*, 1911.

WEBB, WALTER P., *The Texas Rangers*. Boston, Houghton, Mifflin Company, 1935.

WETMORE, HELEN CODY, *Last of the Great Scouts*. New York, Grosset and Dunlap, 1918.

WHEELER, COL. HOMER W., *The Frontier Trail*. Los Angeles, Times-Mirror Press, 1923.

WILLISON, GEORGE F., *Here They Dug the Gold*. New York, Brentano's, 1931.

WILSTACH, F. J., *Wild Bill, the Prince of Pistoleers*. New York, Doubleday, Page & Co., 1926.

Periodicals

CODY, LOUISA FREDERICI (In collaboration with Courtney Riley Cooper) "The Most Thrilling American Romance Ever Told by a Woman," *The Ladies' Home Journal*, June, 1919.

COOPER, COURTNEY RYLEY, "The Story of William Frederick Cody," *The Elks Magazine*, May, 1927.

COURTNEY, W. B., "The Prairie Prince," *Collier's*, April 14, 1928.

MONAGHAN, JAY, "The Stage Career of Buffalo Bill," *Journal of the Illinois State Historical Society*, December, 1938.

NORDIN, CHARLES R., "Dr. W. F. Carver . . . 'Evil Spirit of the Plains,'" *Nebraska History Magazine*, Oct.-Dec., 1927.

GAITHER, RICE, "Then—'Another Redskin Bit the Dust,'" *The New York Times Magazine*, January 4, 1931.

MOORE, LILLIAN, "Ballerina and Plainsman," *Dance Magazine*, September, 1947.

MILLER, ERNEST I., "Ned Buntline," *Bulletin of the Historical and Philosophical Society of Ohio*, January, 1952.

McMECHEN, EDGAR C., "The Tabor Story," *State Historical Society of Colorado*, 1952.

HUNTER, J. MARVIN, "John B. Omohundro, 'Texas Jack',", *Frontier Times*, September, 1941.

ROGERS, BETTY BLAKE, "Uncle Clem's Boy," *The Saturday Evening Post*, October, 1940.

Spirit of the Times, April 5, 1873.

Newspapers

The Age (Philadelphia), April 22, 1873.

The Albany Argus (N. Y.), Feb. 5-6, 1873; Feb. 23, 24, 26, 27, 28, 1874.

The Boston Daily Globe, March 4-5, 1873.

Boston Daily Traveler, March 6, 1873.

Boston Evening Transcript, March 4, 1873.

Boston Herald, Nov. 12, 1911.

Boston Journal, March 4, 1873.

The Chicago Times, Dec. 15, 1872.

Cincinnati Daily Gazette, Dec. 30-31, 1872.

The Daily Chronicle (Leadville, Colo.), June 28, 1880.

The Daily News (Denver), July 1, 1880.

Herald Democrat (Leadville, Colo.), June 29, 1880; Sept. 1-6, 1908.

Lowell Daily Citizen (Mass.), July 24, 1886.

Milwaukee Sentinel, May 2-7, 1874.

New York Herald, Sept. 30, 1876; Feb. 19, 1878.

New York Herald-Tribune, Oct., 1933.

New York Weekly, Nov., 1872-Nov., 1873.

The Norfolk Journal (Virginia), May 14, 15, 16, 17, 18, 1873.

Portland Advertiser (Maine), Jan. 26-30, 1874.

Portland Daily Press (Maine), Jan. 24, 26, 27, 28, 29, 30, 1874.

Richmond Wig (Virginia), April 30, 1873; May 7, 9, 10, 12, 13, 14, 15, 16, 1873.

Richmond Enquirer (Virginia), May 4-9-15, 1873.

Richmond Times-Dispatch (Virginia), Dec. 9, 1951.

Rochester Daily Union and Advertiser (N. Y.), Aug. 20, 1873; Sept. 1, 1873; March 10, 11, 12, 1874.

Rochester Democrat and Chronicle (N. Y.), Sept. 1, 1873; March 13, 1874.

Rocky Mountain News (Denver), March 16-24, 1880.

Syracuse Daily Courier (N. Y.), Nov. 20-21, 1874.

Titusville Morning Herald (Penna.), Nov. 4, 1873.

The Weekly Herald (Omaha, Nebr.), Jan. 17-24, 1872.

ACKNOWLEDGMENTS

It is with a deep sense of gratitude that I express my sincere appreciation to individuals and organizations for their kind and courteous assistance in the preparation of this work. Without such help and cooperation the gathering of much valuable data would have been all but impossible.

The kindness of Libraries, Historical Societies, the National Archives, Newspapers, etc., in permitting the photostating of important documents has aided materially in the compiling of interesting biographical material. To these organizations, and individuals, I wish to extend my heartfelt thanks:

Adjutant General, U. S. Army . . . Maj. Gen. Wm. E. Bergin.

Benson Memorial Library (Penna.) . . . Ruth F. Doty.

Boston Public Library . . . Richard G. Hensley.

Buffalo Bill's Memorial Museum . . . Mrs. "Johnny" Baker.

Brown Brothers . . . Harry B. Collins.

Colorado Historical Society . . . Frances Shea.

Cincinnati Public Library . . . Ethel B. Hutchins.

Denver Public Library, Western History Dept. . . . Mrs. Alys Freeze, and Mrs. Opal Harber.

George Eastman House . . . Beaumont Newhall.

Elks Club (Leadville) . . . Steve Hopko, Buck Glenn.

Frontier Times Museum . . . J. Marvin Hunter.

Iowa State Dept. of History and Archives . . . Claude R. Cook.

Department of the Interior (U. S.) . . . Lem Banks.

Illinois State Historical Society . . . Harry E. Pratt.

Kansas State Historical Society . . . Helen M. McFarland.

Library of Congress . . . Frederick R. Goff, Donald C. Holmes.

Lowell City Library (Mass.) . . . Hugh Downs.

Milwaukee Public Library . . . Ester G. Hamilton.

National Archives and Records Service . . . Richard G. Woods and Oliver W. Holmes.

Nebraska State Historical Society . . . John B. White.

Newberry Library (Chicago) . . . Ben C. Bowman.

New York Public Library . . . Paul North Rice and John A. Gault.

New York World-Telegram . . . Lauretta Ravenna.
New York State Library (Albany) . . . Evelyn Nelson.
Norfolk Public Library (Va.) . . . Mary C. Brown.
Oklahoma Historical Society . . . Elsie D. Hand.
Omaha Public Library . . . Arthur H. Parsons, Jr.
Free Library of Philadelphia . . . Emerson Greenaway.
Portland Public Library (Maine) . . . Eugenia M. Southard.
Rochester Public Library (N. Y.) . . . Emma B. Swift.
Will Rogers Memorial (Okla) . . . Paula M. Love.
Salina Public Library (Kans.) . . . Alice Miller, Mrs. R. H. Turtle and Jerome Cushman.
St. Louis Public Library . . . Mildred Boatman.
Syracuse Public Library (N. Y.) . . . M. Frances Ferris.
Texas State Historical Ass'n . . . H. Bailey Carroll.
Virginia State Library . . . Milton C. Russell.
Union Pacific Railroad (Omaha) . . . Edwin C. Schafer.

And to these individuals many of whom have given most generously of their time, or who have furnished photographs or other items, to assist in this biography I am deeply grateful. To each a sincere, Thank You: Wanda Bloyd, whose excellent camera work made possible the inclusion of much valuable illustrative material, Raymond L. Caldwell, Gertrude W. Crane, Ralph F. Cummings, Selina M. Dermody, Brummett Echohawk, Earle R. Forrest, Ed C. Gunnerson, Dr. G. L. Howe, George Jelinek, Albert Johannsen, William F. Kelleher, Russell Langford, J. Edward Leithead, Sam Logan, North McArthur, W. H. McDonald, Kirke Mechem, Jay Monaghan, W. H. Montgomery, Lillian Moore, Charles R. Nordin, Arthur Omohundro, J. B. Omohundro, M. H. Omohundro, Charles D. Randolph "Buckskin Bill," R. D. Rasmusson, Fred Rosenstock, Don Russell, Peggy and Wayne Sondergard, Howard D. Scott, James E. Serven and Dr. A. Warren Stearns.

INDEX

De Pol's Grand Ballet Troupe

AT THE THEATRE COMIQUE.

Mlles. MORLACCHI AND BARETTA

No. 1. CANCAN.   No. 2. BEE DANCE.   No. 3. BOLERO

by

A. Predigam

BOSTON
G. D. RUSSELL & CO. Tremont St.

ST LOUIS
J. H. KEITH & COMPANY